WHICH IS
NOT TRUE?

—

The Quiz Book

by
Nayden Kostov

WHICH IS NOT TRUE?

—

The Quiz Book

by

Nayden Kostov

Luxemburg
2016

WHICH IS NOT TRUE? – **The Quiz Book**
first edition

Autor:Nayden Kostov
Design: Yuliya Krumova
Format: 5,25 x 8

All rights reserved.
Copyright 2016 © Nayden Kostov
Cover illustration © Yuliya Krumova

ISBN-13: 978-9995998035
ISBN-10: 9995998033

CONTENTS

Canada

Chapter II – Miscellaneous

PROLOGUE

Following the success of my website www.RaiseYourBrain.com and numerous requests from followers, I decided to compile some of the most interesting facts into a book. Earlier this year, the crowdfunding community helped me to publish my book '1123 Hard to Believe Facts'. In and out of the top 10 on multiple Amazon markets and with plenty of 5-star reviews, it is a huge success.

My goal was to write a quiz book that would stand out with interesting, educational and fun content; a book that would both entertain and challenge. The concept is based on the well-known multiple choice format, with an added twist by introducing the 'Which is not true?' approach for half of the quizzes. This approach has its merit in allowing you to learn two crazy facts about people, places or animals by answering a single question.

The book is not meant to be 'your go-to' book for facts. I assure you however that it is loaded with fun and verified facts presented in a manner that can provide you with hours of entertainment. All the material is fresh, and is not simply recycled from my previous publication. Life is too short to settle for the run-of-the-mill. This book will show you just how fantastical and funny the real world is. It will provide you with never-ending intellectual ammunition for a lifetime of dinner parties. You can use it to organise pub or family quizzes, or use it as a prep tool to give you the edge when participating in these.

The book will be a strong and faithful ally preventing social awkwardness by arming you with plenty of icebreaking pieces of trivia, suitable for any occasion.

CHAPTER I

COUNTRIES AND PEOPLE

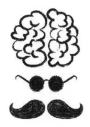

United Kingdom

Quiz 1 – Laws and legal system

1. In Medieval England, 'impersonating an Egyptian'
   a) was considered a serious crime and given the death sentence.
   b) was a wide-spread entertainment practice.
   c) was a way to demonstrate social status.

2. From the 12th century until the 15th century, the main oral language during court trials was
   a) Latin.
   b) Norman French.
   c) Gaelic.

3. Alcohol is prohibited in the House of Commons chamber.
   a) False
   b) True
   c) True with the following exception: the Chancellor is allowed to drink while delivering the annual budget statement.

4. In 1896, the first speeding ticket was issued in East Peckham, Kent, for driving at 13 km/h (8 mph) in a 3.2 km/h (2 mph) zone. The offender's car was pulled over by a policeman who was
   a) running.

b) riding a bicycle.

c) riding a horse.

5. The last state prisoner kept in the Tower of London was

a) Queen Mary II of England.

b) the Nazi Rudolf Hess.

c) Thomas Cromwell.

6. Slavery was banned in 1833. However, it was legally defined as an offence in

a) 1910.

b) 2010.

c) 2015.

7. In the UK, one is deemed fit for voluntary military service at the age of

a) 16.

b) 17.

c) 18.

8. In Scotland, three verdicts for a criminal trial are possible: 'guilty', 'not guilty' and

a) 'guilty, but repented'.

b) 'guilty and no remorse shown'.

c) 'not proven'.

9. The Queen retains the ability to fire the entire Australian government, but

a) it never happened.

b) it last happened in 1975.

c) it last happened in 1988.

10. In 2015, the UK became the first country to allow the creation of babies from the DNA of

a) three people.

b) humans and apes.

c) deceased people.

11. Soldiers in the British Army were required to grow moustaches from 1856 until

a) 1889.

b) 1916.

c) 1923.

Answers:

1. **a.** *THE WANDERING people, called by themselves Romany, first appeared in England in the early 16ᵗʰ century and were then thought to have come from Egypt. Hence the description 'Egyptians' (and its corruption into 'gypsy') and the legislation against them. Thus in 1530 Henry VIII expelled the 'outlandish people calling themselves Egyptians ... who used great, subtil and crafty means to deceive the people ... that they by palmestry could tell men's and women's fortunes'. Later legislation provided that if any 'Egyptians shall remain in this realm or Wales one month ... it is felony', and it was also felony to disguise oneself as an Egyptian or to be seen in company with them.*
2. **b.**
3. **c.**
4. **b.** *A policeman on bicycle pictured below.*

5. **b.**
6. **b.** *Section 71 of the Coroners and Justice Act 2009 introduced a new offence of holding someone in slavery or servitude, or requiring a person to perform forced or compulsory labour. It came into force on 6 April 2010.*
7. **a.**
8. **c.**
9. **b.** *The 1975 Australian constitutional crisis, also known simply as the Dismissal, has been described as the greatest political and constitutional crisis in Australian history. It culminated on 11 November 1975 with the dismissal from office of the Prime Minister, Gough Whitlam of the Australian Labor Party, by Governor-General Sir John Kerr. The Governor-General of the Commonwealth of Australia is the representative in Australia of the Australian monarch, currently Queen Elizabeth II.*
10. **a.**
11. **b.**

United Kingdom
Quiz 2 – The first ever…

1. The first British phonebook contained
   a) 26 names.
   b) 110 names.
   c) 248 names.

2. The London 2012 Olympics were the first Olympics at which every country fielded at least
   a) one female athlete.
   b) two female athletes.
   c) three female athletes.

3. The first fish and chips restaurant opened in
   a) 1784.
   b) 1860.
   c) 1891.

4. Margaret Thatcher became UK's first female prime minister in
   a) 1977.
   b) 1979.
   c) 1981.

5. The first-ever international football match was played between England and Scotland in
   a) 1872.
   b) 1875.
   c) 1880.

6. The first 18-hole golf course was created in St Andrews, Scotland, in
   a) 1754.
   b) 1857.
   c) 1886.

7. The world's oldest tennis tournament, Wimbledon, first took place in
   a) 1877.
   b) 1892.
   c) 1900.

8. The first petrol engine car accident with casualties occurred in London. It happened in
   a) 1894.
   b) 1895.
   c) 1896.

9. Margaret Thatcher was the first British Prime Minister

   a) with a science degree.

   b) to hold a patent.

   c) to have composed a symphony.

10. Concentration camps were first used by the British during the

   a) Crimean War.

   b) Second Anglo-Boer War.

   c) Great War (WW I).

11. J. K. Rowling, the author of the Harry Potter series, became the first author worldwide to break which sales record?

   a) 100 million pounds.

   b) 500 million pounds.

   c) one billion pounds.

WHICH IS NOT TRUE?
The Quiz Book

Answers:

1.   **c.** *It was published in 1880.*
2.   **a.**
3.   **b.**
4.   **b.** *Photo below.*

5.   **a.**
6.   **b.**
7.   **a.**
8.   **c.** *An English lady was run over by a car, travelling at 15 km/h (9 mph).*

9.   **a.** *She earned a degree in chemistry in 1947, and went on to work as a research chemist in Colchester. Later, she worked as a research chemist in Dartford.*

10.   **b.**

11.   **c.**

by Nayden Kostov

United Kingdom

Quiz 3 – When, who, how many…?

1. Stonehenge was erected more than
   a) 2000 years ago.
   b) 3000 years ago.
   c) 4000 years ago.

2. The union between England and Wales started in
   a) 1276.
   b) 1284.
   c) 1364.

3. The Great Fire of London which occurred in 1666 was immensely destructive but the death toll was only
   a) 4 fatalities.
   b) 6 fatalities.
   c) 8 fatalities.

4. The Act of Union that created the United Kingdom of Great Britain from Scotland and England was signed in
   a) 1707.
   b) 1711.
   c) 1723.

5. British ships transported from Africa to the West Indies at least

    a) 100 000 slaves.

    b) two million slaves.

    c) ten million slaves.

6. The Kingdom of Great Britain and the Kingdom of Ireland formally unified in

    a) 1789.

    b) 1796.

    c) 1800.

7. The shortest war the UK has fought in was the Anglo-Zanzibar War of 1896. Zanzibar surrendered after:

    a) 38 minutes of hostilities.

    b) 3 hours of hostilities.

    c) 17 hours of hostilities.

8. After the World War I, the British Empire covered 20 percent of the world's land surface and represented about

    a) 15 percent of the world population.

    b) 25 percent of the world population.

    c) 35 percent of the world population.

9. The independent Republic of Ireland seceded from the United Kingdom in

a) 1918.
b) 1921.
c) 1923.

10. In 1936, King Edward VIII abdicated
   a) after he unsuccessfully tried to limit the power of the Parliament.
   b) as he was a Nazi sympathiser and did not want to lead the country in a possible war against Hitler.
   c) as he wanted to marry an American divorcée.

11. Great Britain returned its former colony Hong Kong to China in
   a) 1978.
   b) 1997.
   c) 2001.

12. On 9 September 2015, Queen Elizabeth II
   a) broke her leg.
   b) became the longest-reigning UK monarch ever, beating Queen Victoria's record.
   c) started paying taxes voluntarily.

13. England has hosted the Summer Olympics
   a) twice.
   b) three times.
   c) four times.

Answers:

1. **c.** *Stonehenge pictured below.*

2. **b.**
3. **b.**
4. **a.**
5. **b.**
6. **c.** *The Acts of Union 1800 (often erroneously referred to as a single Act of Union 1801) united the Kingdom of Great Britain and the Kingdom of Ireland (previously in personal union) to create the United Kingdom of Great Britain and Ireland with effect from 1 January 1801. Both Acts still remain in force in the United Kingdom, but have been repealed in the Republic of Ireland.*

7. **a.** *The cause of the war was the death of the pro-British Sultan Hamad bin Thuwaini on 25 August 1896 and the subsequent succession of Sultan Khalid bin Barghash. The British authorities preferred Hamud bin Muhammed, who was more favourable to British interests, as sultan. In accordance with a treaty signed in 1886, a condition for accession to the sultanate was that the candidate obtain the permission of the British consul, and Khalid had not fulfilled this requirement.*

8. **b.**

9. **b.**

10. **c.**

11. **b.**

12. **b.** *An early photo of Queen Elizabeth II below.*

13. **b.** *1908, 1948 and 2012.*

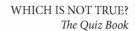

United Kingdom

Quiz 4 – Common misconceptions and rare facts

1. The shortest scheduled flight in the world services a 2.4 km (1.5 miles) distance from Westray to Papa Westray in the Orkney Islands. The flight takes
   a) two minutes.
   b) four minutes.
   c) six minutes.

2. The Hamilton Mausoleum in South Lanarkshire has the longest-lasting echo of any man-made structure world-wide. It lasts
   a) 8 seconds.
   b) 15 seconds.
   c) 28 seconds.

3. Approximately how many umbrellas are lost in London every year?
   a) 100 000.
   b) 300 000.
   c) 500 000.

4. Big Ben refers to the bell inside and not to the famous clock tower. The tower itself is named
   a) the Elizabeth Tower.

b) the Ben Tower.

c) the Egg.

5. The vast majority of portraits of William Shakespeare were painted
   a) by his family members.
   b) by his close friends.
   c) after his death.

6. 30 inhabited localities worldwide and a crater on the moon are named after
   a) Liverpool.
   b) Birmingham.
   c) Glasgow.

7. What do the countries Antigua and Barbuda, Australia, The Bahamas, Barbados, Belize, Canada, Grenada, Jamaica, New Zealand, Papua New Guinea, Saint Kitts and Nevis, Saint Lucia, Saint Vincent and the Grenadines, Solomon Islands, and Tuvalu have in common?
   a) They were all at war with the UK at some point.
   b) The Queen of Great Britain is also their Head of State.
   c) They all broadly use English language, although it is not an official one there.

8. England is 75 times smaller than the USA. It is smaller than the state of

a) North Carolina.

b) Maryland.

c) Vermont.

9. In the early 1800s, 20 percent of the women were named

a) Mary.

b) Elisabeth.

c) Victoria.

10. In the UK, you get a personalised card from the Queen for your

a) 90th birthday.

b) 95th birthday.

c) 100th birthday.

11. In the 14th century, in order to protect them from water-borne diseases many British babies were baptised in

a) wine.

b) cider.

c) beer.

12. On the UK postage stamps you do not normally see

a) their value.

b) the name of the country.

c) the picture of the monarch.

Answers:

1. **a.**

2. **b.**

3. **a.**

4. **a.**

5. **c.**

6. **b.**

7. **b.**

8. **a.** *England has an area of 130 279 km^2 (50 301 sq mi); North Carolina –139 391 km^2 (53 819 sq mi); Maryland – 32 123 km^2 (12 405 sq mi) and Vermont – 24 906 km^2 (9616 sq mi).*

9. **a.**

10. **c.** *The card has to be requested though, it is not automatically sent by the Queen.*

11. **b.** *In the 14th century babies in Herefordshire were baptised in cider, on the grounds that it was cleaner than water. Many people now use the same argument to justify their weekend drinking habits.*

12. **b.**

United Kingdom

Quiz 5 – Random trivia

1. The Beatles are the most commercially successful band in popular music, having sold over

   a)   100 million records.

   b)   300 million records.

   c)   500 million records.

2. One in four London residents is

   a)   Orthodox Christian.

   b)   Muslim.

   c)   foreign-born.

3. What percentage of all restaurants in the UK is located in London?

   a)   10 percent

   b)   17 percent

   c)   25 percent

4. The highest temperature ever recorded in the UK is

   a)   38.5° Celsius (101° Fahrenheit).

   b)   40° Celsius (104° Fahrenheit).

   c)   42.5° Celsius (108.5° Fahrenheit).

5. London has the largest city GDP

   a) in Europe.

   b) worldwide, except for North America.

   c) in the world.

6. The British aerospace industry is the second largest national aerospace industry in

   a) Europe.

   b) Europe, Asia and Africa.

   c) the world.

7. Sir Arthur Conan Doyle (the creator of Sherlock Holmes), Robert Louis Stevenson, and the celebrated poet Robert Burns are all

   a) Welsh.

   b) Scots.

   c) Irish.

8. The London Eye is the tallest Ferris wheel

   a) countrywide.

   b) in Europe.

   c) in the world.

9. Some people believe that a giant monster lives in the Loch Ness, Scotland. Its name is

   a) Nessie.

b) Lessie.

c) Maggie.

10. The maximum distance between any point in Great Britain and the closest coastline is?

a) 120 km (74 miles)

b) 160 km (100 miles)

c) 240 km (148 miles)

11. Which famous music band initially called themselves The Blackjacks and then The Quarrymen?

a) The Beatles

b) Depeche Mode

c) Led Zeppelin

12. The world's best-selling novelist is from the UK; her name is

a) Agatha Christie.

b) Barbara Cartland.

c) J. K. Rowling.

Answers:

1. **c.**
2. **c.**
3. **b.** *McDonald's alone has more than 200 restaurants in the British capital.*
4. **a.**
5. **a.** *London generates 22 percent of the UK's GDP and has the fifth largest city economy in the world, after Tokyo, New York City, Los Angeles and Seoul.*
6. **c.**
7. **b.**
8. **b.**
9. **a.**
10. **a.**
11. **a.** *An early photo of the Beatles below.*

12. **a.**

United Kingdom

Quiz 6 – Weird laws and traditions
(Which is NOT true?)

Two out of every three claims are facts. Can you spot the false fact, the myth, the bullsh*t?

1. Which one is a myth?
    a) It is illegal to die in the Parliament.
    b) It is illegal to ring your neighbour's doorbell and run away.
    c) It is illegal to jump the queue in the tube ticket hall.

2. Which one is a myth?
    a) It is illegal not to carry out at least two hours of long-bow practice a week.
    b) It is illegal to handle salmon in suspicious circumstances.
    c) It is illegal to get drunk in a pub.

3. Which one is a myth?
    a) The British Parliament could, in theory, abolish the Scottish Parliament, the Welsh Assembly and the Northern Ireland Assembly.
    b) The UK does not have a codified constitution.
    c) It is illegal to eat mince pies on Christmas Day.

4. Which one is a myth?

   a) It is illegal to stand within 100 yards of the reigning monarch without wearing socks.

   b) In England, the Speaker of the House cannot speak (he does not participate in debates).

   c) Under the Postal Services Act 2000, it is an offence intentionally to open or delay a postal packet.

5. Which one is a myth?

   a) In the Middle Ages, grave robbing and body snatching was not criminalised in England.

   b) There is still a British law saying it is legal to kill any Scotsman entering the city of York in the possession of a bow and arrow.

   c) All whales and dolphins in the waters within 5 km (3 miles) from the UK coast are property of the crown.

6. Which one is a myth?

   a) Members of Parliament are not allowed to wear armour in Parliament.

   b) No person shall, in the course of a business, import into England potatoes which he knows, or has reasonable cause to suspect, are from Poland.

   c) Any pregnant woman is allowed to urinate in a policeman's helmet.

7. Which one is a myth?

   a) London black cabs must carry a bale of hay and a sack of oats.

   b) It is illegal to carry a plank along a pavement (as well as any ladder, wheel, pole, cask, placard, showboard, or hoop) in the Metropolitan Police District.

   c) It is an offence to beat or shake any carpet, rug, or mat (except door mats before 8 am) in a thoroughfare in the Metropolitan Police District.

8. Which one is a myth?

   a) It is illegal to fire cannon within 300 yards of a dwelling house.

   b) Anyone known to be suffering from plague, may not enter a taxi without first notifying the driver of their ailment.

   c) It is legal for a man to urinate in public, as long it is against the rear offside wheel of his motor vehicle and his right hand is on the vehicle.

9. Which one is a myth?

   a) In bygone times, the rich Britons would allow their less fortunate countrymen to inhabit their newly built houses free of charge whilst the walls dried out.

   b) It is an offence to drive cattle through the streets between 7 pm and 10 am without express permission from the Commissioner of Police.

c) To glue a stamp that has the Monarch's face upside down is considered treason.

10. Which one is a myth?

a) It is illegal to keep a lunatic without a licence.

b) William the Conqueror ordered that everyone should go to bed when a curfew bell was rung.

c) In Scotland, it is illegal to get drunk while carrying a loaded firearm or while in charge of a cow or a horse.

11. Which one is a myth?

a) It is illegal to harbour a Catholic priest.

b) In Medieval times, British animals were tried for their crimes and sometimes executed.

c) All wild, unmarked mute swans in open water are officially owned by the Queen.

Answers:

1. **a.** *It is a persistent myth. One could pass away in the premises of the Parliament without fear of legal consequences.*
2. **a.** *Strangely enough, **b)** is codified in the Salmon Act 1986, and **c)** is a thing since 1872.*
3. **c.** *Festive celebrations, including mince pies and Christmas puddings, were banned in England by Oliver Cromwell (pictured below) for a short period only.*

4. **a.**

5. **b.**

6. **c. a)** *is true since 1313 and **b)** since 2004.*

7. **a.** It was *repealed in 1976.*

8. **c.** *a) is stated in the Metropolitan Police Act 1839 and **b)** in the Public Health Act 1984.*

9. **c.**

10. **a.** *The Madhouses Act 1774 made it an offence. It has now been repealed.*

11. **a.** *Used to be true under the Treason Act 1534, now repealed.*

United Kingdom

Quiz 7 – General knowledge
(Which is NOT true?)

1. Which is false?

a) Pluto is still considered a planet in the UK.

b) 10 000 years ago, Britain was still physically linked to the rest of Europe.

c) UK has three distinct systems of law: English law, Northern Ireland's law and Scottish law.

2. Which is false?

a) Soccer, cricket, rugby, golf, and boxing were all invented in the UK.

b) In the UK, Boxing Day is a bank holiday, celebrated on the day after Christmas. It commemorates the day in which servants used to receive gifts from their employers.

c) England has the highest rate of obesity in Europe.

3. Which is false?

a) People from Liverpool are often called 'Scousers' (short for Lobscouse – a Scandinavian stew, introduced to the city by visiting sailors).

b) The French horn is actually not French at all – it was invented in Manchester.

c) Princess Pocahontas, a daughter of a Native American chieftain, is buried in the UK.

4. Which is false?

a) The oldest human settlement worldwide was discovered in Wales.

b) When Margaret Thatcher died, the song 'Ding Dong! The Witch is Dead' reached the second place in the British radio charts.

c) Mr Smith-Cumming was a head of British Intelligence MI6. Ironically, he introduced a method of using semen as invisible ink.

5. Which is false?

a) Tommy Atkins serves as a generic name for British soldiers.

b) The United Kingdom was the world's first industrialised nation.

c) The neon tube lighting was invented in the UK.

6. Which is false?

a) In 2015, a primary school in the UK banned handstands and cartwheels on health and safety grounds.

b) An inexplicable number of dogs have jumped to their death from Overtoun Bridge near Dunbarton, Scotland. Scientists are yet to identify the cause behind the 'dog suicide' phenomenon.

c) The world's first newspaper was published in London.

7. Which is false?

a) Alessandro Volta invented the battery while living in Scotland.

b) In the UK, it is possible to bet on whether there will be snow on Christmas.

c) In the UK, you can buy trousers with an integrated active carbon filtration system that lessens the strength of your olfactory emissions (i.e. it makes your farts odourless).

8. Which is false?

a) During the first three months of World War II, more Britons died in car accidents in London as a result of the blackout than soldiers in battle.

b) The Welshman Samuel Morse invented the Morse code.

c) In early 2016, a UK man was ordered to give the police 24 hours' prior notice if he intends to have sex.

9. Which is false?

a) The first H-Bomb was detonated on British soil.

b) Nigeria and the Philippines each have more English speakers than the United Kingdom.

c) In July 2015, the UK police were informed of a car accident. It took them three full days to respond. Luckily, the severely injured woman trapped in the wreckage survived.

Answers:

1. **a.** *However, in Illinois, USA, Pluto is a planet. The Illinois State Senate says Pluto was 'unfairly downgraded' to dwarf planet status. In the rest of the world Pluto lost its planetary status in 2006.*

2. **c.** *Andorra currently has the highest percentage of obese population in Europe.*

3. **b.** *Actually, it was most probably invented in Germany. In 1818, the German makers Heinrich Stölzel and Friedrich Blümel patented the first valved horn, using rotary valves. Piston valves were introduced in France about 20 years later. Photo below.*

4. **a.** *The earliest human remains have been dated as ca. 195 000 years old. They were found near the Ethiopian Kibish Mountains.*

5. **c.** *In fact, Georges Claude, a French engineer and inventor, presented neon tube lighting in its modern form at the Paris Motor Show in 1910.*

6. **c.** *The German-language Relation aller Fürnemmen und gedenckwürdigen Historien, printed from 1605 onwards by Johann Carolus in Strasbourg, is often recognized as the first newspaper. At the time, Strasbourg was a free imperial city in the Holy Roman Empire of the German Nation.*

7. **a.**

8. **b.** *Samuel Finley Breese Morse (27 April 1791 – 2 April 1872) was an American painter and inventor.*

9. **a.** *The first H-Bomb was detonated on 1 November 1952 by the United States on Enewetak, an atoll in the Pacific Ocean.*

by Nayden Kostov

United Kingdom

Quiz 8 – Some more general knowledge (Which is NOT true?)

1. Which is false?

a) The first hot chocolate store opened in London.

b) The largest home of any royal family in the world is the Windsor castle.

c) The famous inventor, Nikola Tesla, was born in Oxford.

2. Which is false?

a) London was the first city in the world with an underground system.

b) London Heathrow Airport has more international passenger traffic than any other airport in the world.

c) London used to be called Londinium.

3. Which is false?

a) The UK was the first country in the world to use banknotes.

b) 'The Star Spangled Banner' (the US national anthem) was in fact written by an Englishman.

c) When Prince William and Catherine Middleton got married in 2011, workers and students were given the day off.

4. Which is false?

a) The writer Ian Fleming often took the 007 bus from Canterbury to London. This inspired the code number of his fictional secret agent, James Bond.

b) In the UK, John Smith is one of the most frequent name and surname combinations.

c) Robert Falcon Scott was the first person to reach the South Pole.

5. Which is false?

a) The UK has the most Nobel laureates.

b) All British passports are issued in the Queen's name. This means that she does not herself possess one. She similarly drives without a licence.

c) The national anthem 'God Save the Queen' has the 'Queen' replaced with 'King' whenever the monarch happens to be a man.

6. Which is false?

a) Buckingham Palace has its own post office, police station, chapel, and doctor's surgery.

b) The first steam-powered rail transport was invented in the UK.

c) After the US dollar, the pound sterling is the second largest reserve currency worldwide.

7. Which is false?

a) In 1982, the UK was fought a war 13 000 km (8000 miles) away from London. Britain defeated Argentina and took back the Falkland Islands.

b) After having its membership vetoed twice by France, Great Britain entered the European Economic Community in 1973. In 2016, voters backed the UK exit from the European Union in a referendum.

c) After the WikiLeaks scandals, Julian Assange was stripped of his British citizenship.

8. Which is false?

a) After the end of World War II, over 115 000 Polish veterans settled in the UK permanently as they could not return to Poland.

b) Puerto Rico covers a larger area than Wales.

c) In international rugby competitions Northern Ireland and the Republic of Ireland form one team to represent all of Ireland.

9. Which is false?

a) BBC television is funded by the taxpayer and cannot run commercial adverts.

b) The British Navy used Britney Spears songs to repel Somali pirates.

c) The Republic of Ireland joined the European Economic Community 10 years before the United Kingdom.

Answers:

1. **c.** *Nikola Tesla was born in what is now Croatia.*
2. **b.** *Heathrow was surpassed by Dubai International Airport.*
3. **a.** *Paper bills (pictured below) were first used by the Chinese, who started carrying folding money during the Tang Dynasty (A.D. 618–907) — mostly in the form of privately issued bills of credit or exchange notes — and used it for more than 500 years before the practice began to catch on in Europe in the 17th century.*

4. **c.** *Captain Scott reached the Pole on 17 January 1912, only to find that Roald Amundsen (a Norwegian explorer of the polar regions) had preceded him by five weeks.*
5. **a.** *The UK ranks second, after the USA.*

6. c. *The euro is currently the second most commonly held reserve currency, comprising about a quarter of allocated holdings.*

7. c. *Julian Paul Assange (born 3 July 1971) is an Australian computer programmer, publisher and journalist. He has never been a British citizen.*

8. b. *Puerto Rico – 9104 km² (3515 sq mi) vs Wales – 20 779 km² (8022 sq mi).*

9. c. *Both countries joined the European Economic Community in 1973.*

WHICH IS NOT TRUE?
The Quiz Book

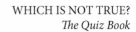

by Nayden Kostov

United States of America
Quiz 1 – Warm-up

1. Which of the following cities is known as the *Rocket City*?
   a) Houston, Texas
   b) Huntsville, Alabama
   c) Colorado Springs, Colorado

2. There are more prisoners in the USA than there are
   a) teachers.
   b) civil servants.
   c) farmers.

3. Which state's nickname is *The First State*?
   a) New York
   b) Pennsylvania
   c) Delaware

4. Which state's motto is *Fatti maschii, parole femine* (*Manly deeds, womanly words*)?
   a) Maryland
   b) New Hampshire
   c) South Carolina

Ready?

Answers:

1. **b.**
2. **c.**
3. **c.** *The flag of Delaware below.*

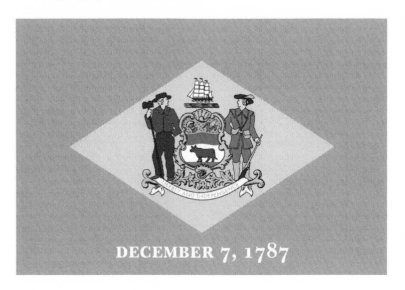

4. **a.**

by Nayden Kostov

United States of America
Quiz 2 – Which is NOT true about the USA?

1. Which is false?

a) Genetically modified salmon was approved for consumption by the US Food and Drug Administration in 2015.

b) Two out of three Americans do not have a passport.

c) It was ascertained by many documents from the Continental Congress that Betsy Ross designed the American flag.

2. Which is false?

a) Charles Lindbergh was the first pilot to fly non-stop over the Atlantic Ocean.

b) Kinder Surprise chocolate eggs are forbidden in the USA.

c) Lew Wallace wrote 'Ben Hur'. He also served as a governor of the US state of New Mexico and once pardoned Billy the Kid.

3. Which is false?

a) During the 1948 Presidential Election, everyone was so sure Thomas Dewey would be elected next US President that the Chicago Daily Tribune splashed the headline 'Dewey Defeats Truman' as its front page before the final results were announced.

b) The founder of KFC, Colonel Sanders, practiced law without a law degree and delivered babies without a medical degree.

c) The cowboy hat became extremely popular in the 1790s.

4. Which is false?

a) Pluto was discovered by Clyde Tombaugh at the Lowell Observatory, Alaska.

b) Over 50 000 Americans get injured in toilets each year.

c) A Cherokee Indian, Sequoyah, aka George Guess, invented their written alphabet - a rare case in recorded history when an illiterate invented an effective writing system.

5. Which is false?

a) The pilgrims did not wear colourful garments.

b) San Francisco, California, has banned the use of plastic water bottles.

c) The shootout scene of the movie 'Heat' is shown to US Marine recruits as an example of how to retreat under enemy fire.

6. Which is false?

   a) Hawaii is the only US state without a straight line on its borders.

   b) Hawaii is the only US state to grow coffee and to use the British Union Jack on its flag.

   c) Hawaii introduced women's suffrage in 1840. Hawaiian women have retained this right ever since.

7. Which is false?

   a) Deaf Americans will be better understood in France than in the UK as the American Sign Language was created by a Frenchman.

   b) The USA was the first country to introduce women's suffrage.

   c) Okay, OK, is a town in Oklahoma.

8. Which is false?

   a) The US Congress can declare a war. Approximately half of the Americans are unaware of this fact.

   b) As of 2016, one in three landline phone calls in the USA are made by robots.

   c) Women were granted the right to vote with the same amendment to the Constitution which repealed the Prohibition.

Answers:

1. **c.** *This fact remains unsupported by any evidence.*

2. **a.** *On 14–15 June 1919, British aviators Alcock and Brown made the first non-stop transatlantic flight. On 21 May 1927, the aviator Charles A. Lindbergh landed his Spirit of St. Louis near Paris, completing the first solo airplane flight across the Atlantic Ocean. The key word here is 'solo'.*

3. **c.** *The cowboy hat gained popularity only in the second half of the 19th century. Below: photo of President Ronald Reagan wearing one.*

4. **a.** *The Lowell Observatory is located in Flagstaff, Arizona.*

5. **a.**

6. **c.**

7. **b.** *New Zealand was the first country to allow women to vote (in 1893). The United States finally began allowing women to vote in 1920, after the ratification of the 19th Amendment to the Constitution.*

8. **c.**

by Nayden Kostov

United States of America
Quiz 3 – The Sad Quiz (Which is NOT true?)
Caution, contains disturbing facts!

1. Which is false?

   a) In 1980, Troy Leon Gregg, a convicted murderer in Georgia, USA, escaped from the prison the night before his execution. He was beaten to death in a bar fight later that night.

   b) Premarital sex is still illegal in all US states.

   c) US women are twice as likely to die from pregnancy and childbirth complications as Canadian women.

2. Which is false?

   a) As of 2015 data, one in nine African American US children has a parent who has been incarcerated.

   b) According to a US report from 2015, human DNA was found in the hot dogs samples of several major brands.

   c) In 2015, more Americans died of diabetes than of cancer.

3. Which is false?

   a) In the USA, garbage collectors die more often at work than police officers.

   b) While the United States represents about 5 percent of the world's population, it houses around 45 percent of the world's prisoners.

c) In the late 1930s, the town of Yaphank, New York, had streets named after Adolf Hitler and Joseph Goebbels.

4. Which is false?

a) A former Disneyland employee, Darreck Enciso, was sentenced in 2015 to one year in prison for attempting to trade Disneyland tickets for sex with an underage girl.

b) In more than 80 percent of the mass shootings in the USA, the killers had obtained their weapons legally.

c) Indianapolis, Indiana, was among the safest cities in the United States in 2015.

5. Which is false?

a) President Ulysses S. Grant had a plan to buy the Dominican Republic for $1.6 million and to send the 4 million recently freed African American slaves there.

b) During the Salem witch trials of 1692, many of those convicted of witchcraft were burnt at the stake.

c) Until 1997, cattle in the US were routinely fed with processed dead cats and dogs. Cattle feed companies bought this key ingredient from cat and dog shelters.

6. Which is false?

a) During the heyday of the Wild West, there was on average one bank robbery every week.

b) In Alabama, the loss of an arm in a work-related accident could make the employer liable to pay up to 49 000 dollars, whereas in Illinois the pay-out limit is 440 000 dollars.

c) In May 2016, the Philadelphia Police Department admitted to having disguised a surveillance SUV as a Google Maps car.

7. Which is false?
   a) As of 2015, Detroit, Michigan, was the most dangerous city in the USA; Irvine, California, was the safest.
   b) 90 percent of all Americans are considered to be obese.
   c) Americans who lived for more than six months in the United Kingdom at any time from 1980 to 1996 are not permitted to donate blood in the United States. Health authorities worry that their blood could spread Mad Cow Disease.

8. Which is false?
   a) Only 10.5 percent of US prison inmates are atheists.
   b) In the US, the total number of prisoners increases by over 1000 individuals each week.
   c) Nearly 70% of deaths on death row in the USA are due to natural causes as a death row inmate would wait an average of 25 years before execution.

9. Which is false?

   a) Each year, more than 30 000 Americans buy an insurance policy, covering the risk 'abdication by aliens'.

   b) Between October 1929, when the Wall Street crash happened, and the end of the year hundreds of suicides were recorded on Wall Street.

   c) The following trademarks are registered today in the USA: Take Yo Panties Off clothing; Dangerous Negro shirts; Midget-Man condoms and inflatable sex dolls; Party With Sluts; Redneck Army apparel; Booty Call sex aids; Dumb Blonde hair products.

10. Which is false?

   a) In 1998, the website of McDonald's (aimed mostly at children) stated that 'Ronald McDonald is the absolute authority in everything'.

   b) In the late 1920s, General Motors secretly started purchasing tram systems in many US cities. Their only aim was to dismantle and replace them with bus lanes.

   c) In the period between the WW I and WW II, the US did not invade another country.

11. Which is false?

   a) The word 'democracy' is not found in the Constitution of the United States of America nor is it present in the Declaration of Independence.

b) The formal abolition of slavery happened 30 years after the end of the Civil War.

c) The town of Woodland, North Carolina, rejected a solar farm project on the basis that they were worried it would 'suck up all the energy from the sun'.

12. Which is false?

a) In 2011, a motorcyclist, Philip A. Contos, attended an anti-helmet rally in Onondaga, New York. Whilst at the rally, he fell off his bike, hitting his head on the pavement. He died from his injuries. According to the police, had he been wearing a helmet, he would have likely lived.

b) Ironically, the very same lawyers that Donald Trump had hired to defend him from the lawsuits by unpaid workers, later sued him for unpaid bills.

c) Benjamin Franklin publicly advocated the turkey over the eagle as the national bird.

13. Which is false?

a) The Declaration of Independence was signed on 4 July 1776.

b) The state of Iowa wants to permit toddlers to use weapons.

c) The United States has the highest incarceration rate in the world.

Answers:

1. **b.**
2. **c.**
3. **b.** *US has 'only' 25 percent of the world's prisoners. Below: prison cells in the notorious Alcatraz.*

4. **c.**
5. **b.** *None of the executed was burnt at a stake.*
6. **a.** *Forget about the Western movies, the real number is much humbler.*
7. **b.** *The real number is about 35 percent.*
8. **c.** *In 2010, a death row inmate waited an average of 178 months (roughly 15 years) between sentencing and execution. Nearly a quarter of deaths on death row in the US are due to natural causes.*
9. **b.** *In fact, there were only several confirmed suicides.*
10. **c.**
11. **b.**
12. **c.** *He did have this idea, but never spoke publicly about it.*
13. **a.** *The signature process actually took several months.*

by Nayden Kostov

United States of America

Quiz 4 – Do you know a thing about Florida?

1. Florida is the 4ᵗʰ most populous state in the United States of America with a population of
    a) 15 million.
    b) 20 million.
    c) 25 million.

2. Florida's population has doubled since
    a) 1970.
    b) 1980.
    c) 1990.

3. The capital city Tallahassee has about
    a) 200 000 residents.
    b) 400 000 residents.
    c) 600 000 residents.

4. Florida deserves its nickname –
    a) the Beach State.
    b) the Sunshine State.
    c) the Flowery State.

5. Lake Okeechobee, Florida, with its 1800 km^2 (700 sq mi) is
    a) the second largest freshwater lake in the United States.

b) the third largest freshwater lake in the United States.

c) the fourth largest freshwater lake in the United States.

6. Florida has more golf courses than any other state, with a total of

a) 300 courses.

b) 1300 courses.

c) 3300 courses.

7. The US city with the most lightning strikes per capita is

a) Miami.

b) Tampa.

c) Clearwater.

8. The population of Florida skyrocketed after the invention of

a) the air conditioning.

b) the fast food.

c) the mosquito repellent.

9. Gatorade was named after

a) the state's official reptile.

b) the University of Florida Gators football team.

c) the cat of its inventor (Gato).

Answers:

1. **b.**
2. **b.**
3. **a.**
4. **b.**
5. **a.**
6. **b.**
7. **c.**
8. **a.**
9. **b.** *Florida Gators' logo below.*

United States of America

Quiz 5 – Really, do you know a thing about Florida?

1. Tony Jannus flew the world's first scheduled passenger flight from St. Petersburg, Florida, to Tampa, Florida, on 1 January
   a) 1914.
   b) 1916.
   c) 1919.

2. In 1944, Miami Beach pharmacist Benjamin Green invented the first
   a) mosquito repellent.
   b) lipstick.
   c) suntan cream.

3. Seven out of the top ten places in the United States with the highest annual average temperature are in Florida. All the rest are in
   a) Hawaii.
   b) California.
   c) Arizona.

4. In 1996, Miami installed the world's first ATM for
   a) skaters.

b) rollerbladers.

c) nudists.

5. With its 300 km (184 miles) local waterways, which place in Florida is also called the 'Venice of America'?
  a) Fort Lauderdale
  b) Tallahassee
  c) Miami

6. Key Largo claims to be the world's
  a) skate capital.
  b) diving capital.
  c) kitesurf capital.

7. Florida is the only state in the USA with two different rivers holding the same name. Both are called the
  a) Manatee River.
  b) Ortega River.
  c) Withlacoochee River.

8. Avocado trees were first planted in Florida as early as
  a) 1833.
  b) 1854.
  c) 1876.

9. Florida is unique in being the only place in the world where crocodiles and alligators

    a) coexist.

    b) are kept as pets.

    c) are both endangered species.

Answers:

1. **a.**
2. **c.**
3. **a.**
4. **b.**
5. **a.** *Fort Lauderdale, photo below.*

6. **b.**
7. **c.**
8. **a.**
9. **a.**

United States of America

Quiz 6 – Florida – Strange laws and events (Which is NOT true?)

1. Which is false?
   a) Florida is the only US jurisdiction where prostitution is legal.
   b) The moonstone is the state's official gem. Ironically, it is not found in Florida, nor was it found on the moon.
   c) In the controversial presidential race of 2000, George W. Bush won with Florida's crucial 25 electoral votes. He won the state with only a few hundred more votes than Al Gore.

2. Which is false?
   a) In 1958, the first US satellite Explorer I was launched from Cape Canaveral.
   b) A museum in Sanibel owns 2 million seashells.
   c) Dwight D. Eisenhower, the 34th President of the United States, was born in Daytona Beach.

3. Which is false?
   a) Florida was the only state to form by separating from a Confederate state.

b) Fort Zachary Taylor in Key West was controlled by the Union during the Civil War and successfully blocked Confederate ships.

c) The Annual Mug Race is the world's longest river sailboat race: 68 km (42 miles) from Palatka to Jacksonville.

4. Which is false?

a) In 1945, the Florida Department of Citrus developed the process for making frozen concentrated orange juice. Now Florida is among the top three orange juice producers worldwide.

b) Cheeseburgers were first served in Pensacola.

c) Florida was the arena of one of the United States' most aggressive 'Indian removal' campaigns – the Seminole Wars.

5. Which is false?

a) The name of Hypoluxo City comes from a Seminole expression meaning 'water all around, no get out'.

b) The alligator is Florida's official state reptile.

c) The song 'Happy Birthday to You' was composed in Orlando.

6. Which is false?

a) It is strictly against the law to have sex with a porcupine in Florida.
b) It is illegal to sell your children in Florida.
c) Florida is the only state in the USA without a McDonald's restaurant within the limits of its state capital.

7. Which is false?
   a) In Florida, touching a manatee is punishable by a $500 fine or jail time.
   b) On Sundays, unmarried women are prohibited from parachuting.
   c) About 95 percent of the US shrimp supply comes from Florida.

8. Which is false?
   a) According to a law in Florida, women are not allowed to break more than three dishes per day.
   b) In terms of population, Tallahassee is the smallest state capital in the USA.
   c) Women risk a fine for falling asleep under a hair dryer.

9. Which is false?
   a) Florida's constitution postulates that pregnant pigs should not be confined in cages.
   b) Florida is the only state to enter the United States by treaty instead of a territorial annexation.

c) In Pensacola, you can only go downtown if you have at least 10 dollars in cash on your person. At the time that it was passed, this law was intended to keep African Americans away from the city centre.

10. Which is false?

a) Florida is the only state outside of the first 13 that uses 'commonwealth' in its name.

b) The 'missionary' position is the only legal sexual position in Florida.

c) It is illegal for husband to kiss his wife's breast in Florida.

11. Which is false?

a) In Destin, selling ice cream in a cemetery is a crime.

b) Florida is the only state that shares its border with just one other state.

c) The motto 'In God We Trust' is widely used in Florida but has never been formally adopted.

Answers:

1. **a.** *Currently, Nevada is the only US jurisdiction to allow legal prostitution.*
2. **c.** *Dwight D. Eisenhower was born on 14 October 1890, in Denison, Texas.*
3. **a.** *West Virginia was the only state to form by separating from a Confederate state.*
4. **b.** *Cheeseburgers were first served in 1934 in Louisville, Kentucky.*
5. **c.** *The origins of 'Happy Birthday to You' date back to at least the late 19th century, when two sisters, Patty and Mildred J. Hill, introduced the song 'Good Morning to All' to Patty's kindergarten class in Kentucky.*
6. **c.**
7. **c.** *Over 90 percent of the seafood consumed in the US is imported from other countries around the world.*
8. **b.** *Montpelier, Vermont, is the least populous US state capital. The population was 7855 at the 2010 census.*
9. **b.**
10. **a.** *The great seal of Florida pictured below.*

11. **b.**

United States of America
Quiz 7 – Florida - when, who, how many…?
(Which is NOT true?)

1. Which is false?

a) Over 7 percent of Florida's total area is water.

b) The highest natural point is only 100 m (345 feet) above sea level.

c) Florida is the largest producer of macadamia nuts and orchids in the world.

2. Which is false?

a) With 2000 km (1300 miles) of coastline, Florida has 1200 km (800 miles) of sand beaches.

b) Florida has almost 20 000 km (12 000 miles) of rivers, streams and waterways.

c) Miami is home to the world's highest roller coaster.

3. Which is false?

a) Florida has 7800 lakes with areas in excess of 10 acres.

b) Florida is the US state with the most numerous first magnitude springs.

c) Until the 1920s, there were grizzly bears living in Florida.

4. Which is false?

a) South Florida boasts average temperatures of over 20° Celsius (68° Fahrenheit) in winter.

b) The six-month hurricane season starts in June.

c) In 1886, Coca-Cola was invented by Dr. John S. Pemberton in Tampa.

5. Which is false?
   a) On average, 1000 people move each day to Florida.
   b) The state has 102 counties.
   c) Greater Miami is the only metropolitan area in the United States that borders with two national parks.

6. Which is false?
   a) Saint Augustine is the oldest continuously inhabited European established settlement in the Continental United States.
   b) In 1862, Richard Gatling invented the rapid-fire machine gun in Orlando.
   c) Orlando is the most visited US amusement park destination.

7. Which is false?
   a) The rapper Flo Rida was not born in Florida.
   b) Almost half of the US exports to Latin America pass through Florida.
   c) Actors Faye Dunaway, Burt Reynolds and Sidney Poitier are Floridians. So is Gloria Estefan.

8. Which is false?

a) Florida is the only state that grows coffee.

b) Any place in Florida is no more than 100 km (60 miles) from the ocean.

c) In 2015, Florida was visited by more than 100 million tourists.

9. Which is false?

a) Florida produces 70 percent of the US oranges and supplies an amazing 40 percent of the world's orange juice.

b) Jimmy Carter, the 39th President, was born in Fort Lauderdale.

c) Florida has no state income tax.

10. Which is false?

a) *'Florida'* means 'flowery' in Spanish.

b) Florida is the southernmost US state.

c) Florida became a US Territory in 1821 with General Andrew Jackson as its military governor.

11. Which is false?

a) In 1989, the Dame Point Bridge became the longest concrete single-span bridge in the Western Hemisphere.

b) Florida has over 100 million citrus trees.

c) There are around one million crocodiles in Florida.

Answers:

1. **c.**

2. **c.** *The world's highest roller coaster has a height of 139 m (456 feet) and is installed in Jackson, New Jersey.*

3. **c.**

4. **c.** *Coca-Cola's history actually started in Atlanta, Georgia.*

5. **b.** *There are 67 counties in the state of Florida.*

6. **b.** *Richard Gatling invented his gun in Indianapolis, Indiana.*

7. **a.**

8. **a.** *The only state in the USA able to grow coffee plants commercially is Hawaii. However, it is not the only coffee grown on US soil as Puerto Rico has had a coffee industry for some time, although it is not a state but a US territory.*

9. **b.** *Jimmy Carter was born on 1 October 1924 in Plains, Georgia.*

10. **b.** *It is Hawaii.*

11. **c.** *In fact, the crocodile (photo below) is an endangered species in Florida, counting less than 3000.*

United States of America
Quiz 8 – Texas trivia

1. 'Don't mess with Texas' first appeared in 1986 as
    a) an anti-litter slogan.
    b) an election slogan.
    c) a Chuck Norris quote.

2. The least populated US County is Loving County. It covers a larger area than Hong Kong and Singapore combined but has only
    a) 95 residents.
    b) 820 residents.
    c) 3205 residents.

3. The first rodeo ever was held in Pecos, in
    a) 1868.
    b) 1883.
    c) 1897.

4. The Galveston hurricane of 1900 is thought to be the deadliest natural disaster in the US, killing around
    a) 3500 people.
    b) 8000 people.
    c) 12 000 people.

5. Texas is widely known as
   a) The Lone Star State.
   b) The Sunshine State.
   c) The Diamond State.

6. At the Alamo, 200 defenders bravely fought to death against
   a) 700 troops led by the Mexican General Santa Anna.
   b) 1200 troops led by the Mexican General Santa Anna.
   c) 2000 troops led by the Mexican General Santa Anna.

7. The Republic of Texas existed from 1836 to
   a) 1845.
   b) 1847.
   c) 1851.

8. Sam Houston was the first president and first governor of Texas. Little known facts: he was born in Virginia and served as governor of
   a) Tennessee.
   b) Oklahoma.
   c) Indiana.

9. Texas is the second most populous state with its
   a) 21 million people.
   b) 27 million people.
   c) 32 million people.

10. In terms of population, Houston, Dallas and San Antonio are all in the US
   a) top 10.
   b) top 15.
   c) top 20.

11. The state's motto is
   a) 'Friendship'.
   b) 'Liberty and Independence'.
   c) 'Esto perpetua'.

12. Caddo Lake is Texas' only
   a) salt-water lake.
   b) lake below the sea level.
   c) natural lake.

13. The first covered stadium in the US was constructed in Houston
   a) in 1965.
   b) in 1970.
   c) In 1975.

14. Texas is the state enduring the largest number of tornadoes – on average
   a) 80 per year.
   b) 140 per year.
   c) 230 per year.

15. If Texas were an independent country (data as of 2015), it would have roughly the same GDP as

a) Germany.

b) Canada.

c) Mexico.

by Nayden Kostov

Answers:

1. **a.**
2. **a.** *(As of 2013)*
3. **a.**
4. **c.**
5. **a.**

6. **c.**
7. **a.**
8. **a.**
9. **b.**
10. **a.**
11. **a.**
12. **c.**
13. **a.**

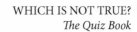

14. **b.**
15. **b.**

United States of America

Quiz 9 – Texas – weird laws and facts
(Which is NOT true?)

1. Which is false?

a) *'Texas'* comes from the Spanish pronunciation of a Hasinai Indian word meaning *'friends'*. Ironically, the Hasinai tribe was completely wiped out.

b) Texas is in the top ten states in terms of percentage of adults without diplomas.

c) Texas produces more oil than Saudi Arabia.

2. Which is false?

a) 'Dallas' TV series ran from 1978 to 1991 and was broadcast in almost 100 countries.

b) In terms of area, Texas is slightly larger than Alaska.

c) Texas had the highest number of prisoner-of-war camps in the WW II – over 70. They housed German, Italian and Japanese soldiers.

3. Which is false?

a) Texas ranks 5th amongst all US states by GDP.

b) John Pershing, Commander of the US Expeditionary Force in World War I, failed to stop Pancho Villa from crossing the border. Villa's troops reached the state of New Mexico before retreating.

c) Amarillo hosts the World's Largest Calf Fry Festival. *'Calf fries'* are, in fact, bull testicles.

4. Which is false?

a) Texas has more obese adults than Wisconsin has people.

b) Texas is known as the *'Silver Star State'*.

c) El Paso is in fact closer to California than it is to Dallas.

5. Which is false?

a) Beaumont is at roughly the same distance from El Paso (both are in Texas), as it is from Chicago, Illinois.

b) Texas is the home of the only active diamond mine in the USA.

c) *'Maverick'* is derived from the name of an early Texan lawyer and pioneer, Samuel Maverick.

6. Which is false?

a) Almost 80 percent of all Snickers bars are made in Waco.

b) The world's largest silver nugget was found in 1894 near Austin.

c) Davy Crockett, the hero from Alamo, said after serving three terms as a Tennessee congressman: *'You all can go to hell. I am going to Texas'*.

7. Which is false?

   a) Texas is the only state to have been ruled by six different nations: Spain, France, Mexico, the Republic of Texas, the Confederate States, and the USA.

   b) Texas was the only state to enter the Union by treaty instead of a territorial annexation.

   c) The longest main street in North America is in Dallas.

8. Which is false?

   a) Texas is home of the largest cave in the world.

   b) The dome of the capitol in Austin stands 2 m (7 feet) higher than the Capitol in Washington, D.C.

   c) Texas has 1000 km (625 miles) of coastline along the Gulf of Mexico.

9. Which is false?

   a) Texas has 254 counties, more than any other state. 41 of them are each larger than the state of Rhode Island.

   b) The oldest fossils in the world were found in Texas.

   c) There are over 1.5 million illegal immigrants in Texas.

Answers:

1. **c.**
2. **b.**
3. **a.** *In terms of GDP, Texas is surpassed only by California.*
4. **b.**
5. **b.** *The only active diamond mine in the country is the Crater of Diamonds Mine near Murfreesboro, Pike County, Arkansas.*
6. **b.** *The world's largest silver nugget (835 kg or 1840 pounds) was pulled out of Smuggler Mine near the city of Aspen, Colorado.*
7. **c.** *The longest main street in North America, stretching 53 km (33 miles), is in Island Park, Idaho.*
8. **a.** *The world's largest cave, Son Doong, is in Vietnam. It is over 9 km (5.5 miles) long, has a jungle and river, and could fit a 40-story skyscraper within its walls. Photo below.*

9. **b.** *The oldest fossils on Earth were discovered in Greenland, in rocks that are believed to be 3.7 billion years old.*

United States of America

Quiz 10 – Texas – more weird laws and facts (Which is NOT true?)

1. Which is false?

a) The first US gasoline automobile was produced in Texas.

b) When Texas joined the Union in 1845, it kept the right to fly its flag at the same height as the national flag.

c) More bat species can be found in Texas than in any other state.

2. Which is false?

a) Dell and Compaq have their headquarters in central Texas, which is often referred to as the Silicon Valley of the South.

b) San Antonio hosts the only roller-skating museum in the world.

c) The first suspension bridge in the US was built in 1870 in Waco and is still operational.

3. Which is false?

a) Guadalupe is the highest peak in Texas with its 2667 m (8751 feet).

b) Dwight D. Eisenhower and Lyndon B. Johnson were the only Texas-born presidents of the USA.

c) Texas is the driest state.

4. Which is false?

   a) Homosexual behaviour is a misdemeanour offence in Texas.

   b) In Odessa, the Star of David and the peace symbol are considered to be satanic symbols and are, thus, prohibited.

   c) Texas has a larger GDP than New York and Illinois combined.

5. Which is false?

   a) Texas is home of the world's first drive-in movie theatre, built in 1933.

   b) There are over 110 000 km (70 000 miles) of highways in Texas.

   c) To be elected in Texas, one must believe in a supreme being.

6. Which is false?

   a) The first electric traffic lights were invented and installed in Austin.

   b) In Texas, pharmacists should abstain from becoming members of the Communist Party.

   c) In Texas, there are 30 000 machine guns in possession of ordinary citizens. There is no gun registry in this state.

7. Which is false?

   a) The world's first parking meter was installed in Dallas.

   b) In Texas, you are considered legally married if you publicly introduce somebody as your spouse three times.

   c) John Wayne and Chuck Norris are both honorary Texas Rangers. The Texas Rangers have state-wide jurisdiction and are the oldest law enforcement agency in North America.

8. Which is false?

   a) In the 19th Century, 'G.T.T.' was a popular abbreviation of 'Gone to Texas'. So many people fled there escaping the law that 'G.T.T.' quickly became a synonym of 'to run off'.

   b) Jane Elkins, a female slave, was the first woman legally executed in Texas, in 1854.

   c) The typewriter was invented in El Paso.

Answers:

1. **a.** *The Duryea Motor Wagon Company, established in 1895 in Springfield, Massachusetts, was the first American firm to build gasoline automobiles.*
2. **b.** *The National Museum of Roller Skating is in Lincoln, Nebraska.*
3. **c.** *The driest state is Nevada.*
4. **c.**
5. **a.** *The drive-in theatre was patented by Richard M. Hollingshead in 1933. He was from Camden, New Jersey.*
6. **a.** *An electric traffic light was developed in 1912 by Lester Wire, a policeman in Salt Lake City, Utah. On 5 August 1914, the American Traffic Signal Company installed a traffic signal system on the corner of East 105th Street and Euclid Avenue in Cleveland, Ohio.*

7. **a.** *In 1935, the world's first parking meters were installed in Oklahoma City, Oklahoma.*
8. **c.** *The first typewriter to be commercially successful was invented in 1868 by Americans Christopher Latham Sholes, Frank Haven Hall, Carlos Glidden and Samuel W. Soule in Milwaukee, Wisconsin, although Sholes soon disowned the machine and refused to use, or even to recommend it.*

United States of America
Quiz 11 – California trivia

1. California became the 31ˢᵗ state in
   a) 1850.
   b) 1852.
   c) 1855.

2. California has a bigger population than
   a) the United Kingdom.
   b) Canada.
   c) Germany.

3. Los Angeles, San Diego and San Jose are all in the top 10
   a) largest US cities.
   b) most dangerous US cities.
   c) US cities where African-Americans are doing the best economically.

4. Several Native American groups lived in California. Among them were:
   a) Cherokee, Chickasaw, Choctaw and Koasati.
   b) Yuma, Maidu, Pomo, Hupa and Paiute.
   c) Apache, Bidai, Coahuiltecan, Caddo and Comanche.

5. Which states are larger than California in terms of territory?
   a) Alaska and Oregon
   b) Alaska and Montana
   c) Alaska and Texas

6. San Bernardino County is the largest county in the USA. It covers nearly
   a) one million acres.
   b) three million acres.
   c) five million acres.

7. Worldwide, California is the
   a) 7th largest economy.
   b) 10th largest economy.
   c) 14th largest economy.

8. California was initially named the Grizzly Bear State. When there were no bears left, it became the
   a) Golden State.
   b) Silver State.
   c) Gem State.

9. California is the only state
   a) to have hosted both Summer and Winter Olympics.
   b) not to have a straight line for a border.

c) to have over 20 million residents.

10. Gold Rush began in 1848, but there was also a Silver Rush in California from
   a) 1851 to 1860.
   b) 1881 to 1896.
   c) 1898 to 1907.

11. Annually, California experiences around
   a) 10 000 earthquakes.
   b) 100 000 earthquakes.
   c) 1 000 000 earthquakes.

12. In 2015, Los Angeles International was the
   a) 2nd busiest passenger airport in the world.
   b) 4th busiest passenger airport in the world.
   c) 7th busiest passenger airport in the world.

13. Jerry Brown was elected twice governor of California: in 1975 and then again in
   a) 1995.
   b) 2005.
   c) 2010.

WHICH IS NOT TRUE?
The Quiz Book

Answers:

1. **a.**
2. **b.**
3. **a.**

4. **b.**
5. **c.**
6. **b.**
7. **a.** *(Estimates for 2016 by International Monetary Fund)*
8. **a.**
9. **a.**
10. **b.**
11. **b.**
12. **c.**
13. **c.**

by Nayden Kostov

United States of America
Quiz 12 – California (Which is NOT true?)

1. Which is false?
   a) The state's official insect is the Monarch butterfly.
   b) Called *'the most corrupt politician in Fresno County history'*, Joseph Spinney was mayor of Fresno for only ten minutes.
   c) During the Gold Rush, miners used to send their laundry to Hawaii for washing and pressing as it was much cheaper compared to local prices.

2. Which is false?
   a) The famous actor John Wayne was born in San Diego.
   b) Most people in California belong to a minority ethnic group.
   c) Every fourth Californian was not born in the US.

3. Which is false?
   a) California grows half of all US fruits and vegetables.
   b) The state's official animal is the sperm whale.
   c) Almonds are the biggest export.

4. Which is false?
   a) Alpine County is very small and has no high school, bank, ATM, dentist or traffic lights.

b) California was the first state in the USA to reach one trillion dollars GDP.

c) California is the state with the largest variety of bat species.

5. Which is false?

a) The lowest and the highest points in the continental US (Death Valley and Mt. Whitney) are both in the state of California.

b) California has both the world's largest and the world's tallest tree.

c) The state's motto means *'Gold and silver'*.

6. Which is false?

a) California's state flag is depicting a real grizzly bear, named Monarch.

b) After Utah, this is the state with the largest Mormon population (in absolute numbers).

c) The state's motto *'Eureka'* dates back to the days of the Gold Rush.

7. Which is false?

a) Arnold Schwarzenegger was a governor of the state.

b) San Francisco Bay is one of the world's biggest land-locked harbours.

c) California is the state with the lowest Adult Obesity Rate.

8. Which is false?

a) Wine industry of California has annual revenues of more than 25 billion dollars.

b) California is the state with the largest cheese production.

c) California grows over 99 percent of all dates in the US.

9. Which is false?

a) The first McDonald's restaurant opened in San Bernardino.

b) In 1947, Norma Jean Baker, later known as Marilyn Monroe, was crowned Artichoke Queen in Castroville.

c) The mockingbird is California's official bird.

Answers:

1. **a.** *The California dogface butterfly or dog head (Zerene eurydice) was designated the official State Insect in 1972.*
2. **a.** *The actor John Wayne was born Marion Robert Morrison on 26 May 1907, in Winterset, Iowa.*
3. **b.** *The California grizzly bear (Ursus californicus) was designated as the official state animal of California in 1953 (more than 30 years after the last one was killed). California's state flag is depicting a real grizzly bear, named Monarch.*

4. **c.** *Texas has the highest bat diversity of all the states – more than 30 bat species.*
5. **c.** *The state motto of California is 'Eureka'. It translates from Greek 'I have found it'.*
6. **b.**
7. **c.**

8. b. *Wisconsin's nickname as 'America's Dairyland' punctuates the state's leading position within the US dairy industry. California is the second largest producer.*
9. c. *California designated the California valley quail as official state bird in 1931.*

United States of America
Quiz 13 – New York trivia

1. Until 1664, New York City's name was
   a) New Albany.
   b) New Harlem.
   c) New Amsterdam.

2. Queens, Bronx, Staten Island and Brooklyn joined Manhattan to form a *'Greater New York'* in 1898, doubling the population and expanding the territory
   a) 4 times.
   b) 6 times.
   c) 8 times.

3. The state of New York first introduced license plates for
   a) cars.
   b) bicycles.
   c) airplanes.

4. New York City (NYC) has a bigger population than
   a) 50 percent of US states.
   b) 65 percent of US states.
   c) 80 percent of US states.

5. A taxi license in NYC costs up to
   a) $10 000.

b) $100 000.

   c) $1 million.

6. The capital Albany was founded by Dutch settlers and was originally named
  a) Fort Orange.
  b) New Leiden.
  c) New Utrecht.

7. Presidents Martin Van Buren, Theodore Roosevelt, Franklin Delano Roosevelt and Millard Fillmore were all
  a) born in this state.
  b) elected mayor of NYC.
  c) elected Attorney General of New York.

8. The first American railroad connected Albany with
  a) Schenectady.
  b) Troy.
  c) Kingston.

9. New York joined the Union on 26 July 1788. It was
  a) the 11th state.
  b) the 12th state.
  c) the 13th state.

10. Pinball was banned in NYC until

a) 1968.

b) 1976.

c) 1988.

11. A hot dog stand annual permit in Central Park can cost over

a) $30 000.

b) $100 000.

c) $300 000.

12. The East River's name is misleading – it is technically not

a) a river.

b) in the east of NYC.

c) even partially on NYC territory.

13. Washington Square Park, Madison Square Park, Bryant Park and Union Square Park all used to be

a) cemeteries.

b) junkyards.

c) weapon test sites.

14. The Federal Reserve Bank on Wall Street holds about

a) 10 percent of the world's gold.

b) 25 percent of the world's gold.

c) 35 percent of the world's gold.

15. How many Chinese food carton boxes are used every year in New York City?

a) 10 million

b) 100 million

c) 300 million

Answers:

1. **c.**
2. **b.**
3. **a.**
4. **c.** *Photo of New York City below.*

5. **c.**
6. **a.**
7. **a.**
8. **a.**
9. **a.**
10. **b.** *Pinball was banned beginning in the early 1940s until 1976 in New York City. New York mayor Fiorello La Guardia was responsible for the ban, believing that it robbed school children of their hard earned nickels and dimes.*
11. **c.**
12. **a.**
13. **a.**
14. **b.**
15. **b.**

United States of America
Quiz 14 – New York (Which is NOT true?)

1. Which is false:

   a) New York City (NYC) was for a while the first capital of the United States of America.

   b) The people of France sent the Statue of Liberty to the American people as a present.

   c) In the state of New York, you can buy liquor in a grocery store.

2. Which is false:

   a) There are over 1000 km (more than 700 miles) of subway lines in New York City.

   b) Women cannot go topless in New York City.

   c) About 1 in every 37 people living in the USA is a New York City resident.

3. Which is false:

   a) Niagara Reservation became the first state park in the United States.

   b) In 1906, the Bronx Zoo exhibited a human being in a cage – a Congolese pygmy named Ota Benga.

   c) In 2006, New York legalised heroin to drop down the incarceration rate.

4. Which is false:

a) There is not a single Walmart store in New York City.

b) Usama Bin Laden was wanted by the FBI for the 9/11 attacks.

c) Farting in New York City churches is considered a misdemeanour.

5. Which is false:

a) New York is the state with the lowest obesity rate.

b) The 'New York Post' is the oldest running newspaper in the country.

c) In 1945, a B-25 bomber slammed into the Empire State Building.

6. Which is false:

a) Hog Island, a one-mile-long island close to NYC, disappeared overnight during the hurricane of 1893.

b) New York is the state with the largest population.

c) On 28 November 2012, not a single incident of violent crime was reported in NYC.

7. Which is false:

a) Queens is referred to as *'the home of jazz'*.

b) NYC has the largest stock exchange in the world.

c) In 2013, New York was named *'the most depressing state'*.

Answers:

1. **c.**
2. **b.** *Women may go topless in public, providing it is not being used as a business.*
3. **c.**
4. **b.** *Usama Bin Laden's Most Wanted poster (pictured below) did not make any direct connection with the events of 11 September 2001. Instead, the FBI said on its Bin Laden web page that he was wanted in connection with the 7 August 1998 bombings of the United States Embassies in Dar es Salaam, Tanzania, and Nairobi, Kenya.*

FBI TEN MOST WANTED FUGITIVE

Murder of U.S. Nationals Outside the United States; Conspiracy to Murder U.S. Nationals Outside the United States; Attack on a Federal Facility Resulting in Death

USAMA BIN LADEN

Date of Photograph
Unknown

Aliases:
Usama Bin Muhammad Bin Ladin, Shaykh Usama Bin Ladin, the Prince, the Emir, Abu Abdallah, Mujahid Shaykh, Hajj, the Director

DESCRIPTION

Date(s) of Birth Used:	1957	Hair:	Brown
Place of Birth:	Saudi Arabia	Eyes:	Brown
Height:	6' 4" to 6' 6"	Complexion:	Olive
Weight:	Approximately 160 pounds	Sex:	Male
Build:	Thin	Nationality:	Saudi Arabian
Occupation:	Unknown		

Scars and Marks: None known
Remarks: Bin Laden is the leader of a terrorist organization known as Al-Qaeda, "The Base". He is left-handed and walks with a cane.

CAUTION

Usama Bin Laden is wanted in connection with the August 7, 1998, bombings of the United States Embassies in Dar es Salaam, Tanzania, and Nairobi, Kenya. These attacks killed over 200 people. In addition, Bin Laden is a suspect in other terrorist attacks throughout the world.

REWARD

The Rewards For Justice Program, United States Department of State, is offering a reward of up to $25 million for information leading directly to the apprehension or conviction of Usama Bin Laden. An additional $2 million is being offered through a program developed and funded by the Airline Pilots Association and the Air Transport Association.

CONSIDERED ARMED AND EXTREMELY DANGEROUS

If you have any information concerning this person, please contact your local FBI office or the nearest American Embassy or Consulate.
June 1999 Poster Revised November 2001

5. **a.**

6. **b.** *California is the most populous state in the USA with over 38 million residents, twice as many as New York.*

7. **c.**

United States of America

Quiz 15 – What do you know about George Washington, the first US President?

1. Some argue that George Washington was NOT the first US president – most probably having in mind
   a) John Hanson.
   b) John Hancock.
   c) Alexander Hamilton.

2. Has George Washington ever been elected unanimously by the Electoral College?
   a) No
   b) Yes, once
   c) Yes, twice

3. George Washington set a record by pronouncing his inaugural address in less than
   a) 2 minutes.
   b) 4 minutes.
   c) 6 minutes.

4. George Washington was inaugurated in two different cities: New York City and
   a) Washington D.C.
   b) Philadelphia.
   c) Baltimore.

5. How many new states joined during Washington's Presidency?

   a) 1

   b) 5

   c) 9

6. In 1793, George Washington

   a) endorsed the Fugitive Slave Act, making it a federal crime to assist a runaway slave.

   b) created the United States Navy.

   c) established a 6-member Supreme Court and the position of Attorney General.

7. Since 1896, the Senate commemorates Washington's birthday

   a) with fireworks that last 45 minutes.

   b) with a cocktail, inviting 30 handpicked homeless people from the D.C. area.

   c) with an annual reading aloud of the full text of his Farewell Address, by a selected sitting Senator.

8. Which animals did he love most, just like members of the family?

   a) Hound dogs

   b) Cats

   c) Turtles

Answers:

1. **a.**
2. **c.**

3. **a.**
4. **b.**
5. **b.**
6. **a.**
7. **c.**
8. **a.**

United States of America

Quiz 16 – George Washington
(Which is NOT true?)

1. Which is false?

a) George Washington was a rich man – his assets would amount today to more than $500 million.

b) He did not retire definitely. In 1798, he came out of retirement when there was a possibility of a war with France.

c) He made Christmas a federal holiday.

2. Which is false?

a) George Washington was obsessed with cats.

b) He introduced the cabinet of advisors.

c) The first copyright law was enacted during his Presidency.

3. Which is false?

a) George Washington owned 800 slaves and established a system that ensured that escapees were returned to their masters.

b) George Washington had to surrender once during a battle.

c) After his second term of office, George Washington ran for the US Senate.

4. Which is false?

  a) Toothaches tortured George Washington for many years. At the age of 57, he had all his teeth extracted.

  b) Like other farmers, he grew hemp as a cash crop, but did not smoke for pleasure.

  c) He was fluent in Arabic.

5. Which is false?

  a) George Washington agreed to pay an annual tribute to the Pasha of Tripoli in exchange for safe access to the Mediterranean shipping lanes.

  b) He was contemplating to buy Alaska from the Russian Emperor.

  c) The dollar became an official currency during his term of office.

6. Which is false?

  a) Washington did not have children of his own and unfortunately lost two stepchildren.

  b) He was the first US President to visit a federal prison.

  c) He never lived in Washington D.C.

Answers:

1. **c.** *President Ulysses S. Grant declared Christmas a legal holiday in 1870.*
2. **a.**
3. **c.**
4. **c.**
5. **b.**
6. **b.** *The first US President to visit a federal prison was Barack Obama (photo below).*

United States of America
Quiz 17 – Abraham Lincoln

1. Abraham Lincoln
- a) had no middle name and actually hated being called Abe.
- b) tried to conceal the fact that his middle name was *'Molly'*.
- c) had simply a *'B.'* instead of a middle name.

2. Lincoln was the first US president to
- a) possess no slaves while in office.
- b) be on a postage stamp.
- c) have a beard.

3. Abraham Lincoln ran twice for the US Senate and
- a) lost both.
- b) lost the first time.
- c) was successful in both elections.

4. Abraham Lincoln was the first President of the United States to
- a) host an Indian Chief in the White House.
- b) visit the Holy Land.
- c) be assassinated.

5. Lincoln was a great wrestler: out of 300 matches he lost

    a) none.

    b) 1.

    c) 2.

6. Abraham Lincoln was obsessed with

    a) cats.

    b) dogs.

    c) alligators.

7. He made a national holiday of

    a) Christmas.

    b) Thanksgiving.

    c) 4 July.

8. Booth's original plan was not to kill the President but

    a) to kidnap him.

    b) to smear him with faeces.

    c) to cut his beard.

Answers:

1. a.

2. **c.**
3. **a.**
4. **c.**
5. **b.**
6. **a.**
7. **b.**
8. **a.**

United States of America

Quiz 18 – Abraham Lincoln
(Which is NOT true?)

1. Which is false:

  a) In 1862, Abraham Lincoln personally endorsed the largest mass hanging in US history, which led to the hanging of 38 Dakota Indian men in Minnesota.

  b) Lincoln was the first President to shake hands instead of bow.

  c) Edwin Booth, a brother of Lincoln's assassin, saved the life of President Lincoln's son in a train accident.

2. Which is false:

  a) So far, Abraham Lincoln is the only President to have held a patent.

  b) Lincoln was the first President to ride on a train.

  c) Lincoln set up the Department of Agriculture.

3. Which is false:

  a) Abraham Lincoln was the first President to have a Christmas Tree in the White House.

  b) He established a standardised currency and the national banking system.

  c) The first president to use the telegraph, Lincoln exchanged daily messages with his generals.

4. Which is false:

   a) Lincoln introduced the nation's first income tax.

   b) He read the Bible but never belonged to any church.

   c) He was the first President to have a stove in the White House.

5. Which is false:

   a) Abraham Lincoln endorsed legislation, which in fact created the US Secret Service only few hours before his assassination.

   b) He was the first President to meet the Queen of England.

   c) He never actually used what is known today as the Lincoln Bedroom in the White House.

6. Which is false:

   a) During the Civil War, Lincoln severely violated civil liberties throughout the Union. He simply ignored court rulings which stated that he had exceeded his constitutional powers.

   b) Several massacres of Indians took place during his term of office.

   c) He was the first unmarried man to be elected President.

by Nayden Kostov

Answers:

1. **b.** *Thomas Jefferson was the first President to shake hands instead of bow.*
2. **b.** *Andrew Jackson was the first President to ride on a train.*
3. **a.** *Benjamin Harrison was the first President to have a Christmas Tree in the White House.*
4. **c.** *Millard Fillmore was the first President to have a bathtub with running water. He was also the first President to have a stove in the White House.*
5. **b.** *U.S. Grant was the first president to meet the Queen of England.*
6. **c.** *James Buchanan (picture below) was the first unmarried man to be elected President.*

Canada

Quiz 1 – Trivia pursuit

1. John Cabot was thought to be the first explorer to reach Canada in 1497. In reality, the East Coast of Canada had been discovered five centuries before by the
   a) Vikings.
   b) Normans.
   c) Babylonians.

2. Alberta has half of the world's deposits of
   a) bitumen.
   b) diamonds.
   c) uranium.

3. The British Parliament endorsed the British North America Act, thus creating Canada as a federal dominion in
   a) 1867.
   b) 1871.
   c) 1876.

4. The French explorer, Jacques Cartier, mistakenly thought the name of the country was *'Kanata'* or Canada as locals invited him to their *'kanata'*, meaning
   a) 'village'.
   b) 'house'.

c) 'shrine'.

5. Canada enjoys a literacy rate of
    a) 90 percent.
    b) 95 percent.
    c) 99 percent.

6. Canada has a population density of
    a) 3 people per km^2 (10 per sq mile).
    b) 30 people per km^2 (100 per sq mile).
    c) 300 people per km^2 (1000 per sq mile).

7. Almost a quarter of the population in Canada is
    a) foreign born.
    b) indigenous people.
    c) former illegal immigrants.

8. Canada has six time zones and is
    a) the largest country in the world.
    b) the second largest country in the world.
    c) the third largest country in the world.

9. The Bay of Fundy in New Brunswick has the highest tides in
    a) Canada.
    b) North America.

c) the world.

10. Worldwide, Ottawa is amongst the top ten
   a) coldest capitals.
   b) most sparsely populated capitals.
   c) most polluted capitals.

11. Canada has the longest coastline in the world. It is roughly
   a) two times longer than the equator.
   b) six times longer than the equator.
   c) ten times longer than the equator.

Answers:

1. **a.** *John Cabot is pictured below.*

2. **a.**
3. **a.**
4. **a.**
5. **c.**
6. **a.**
7. **a.**
8. **b.** *Russia is the largest country in the world.*
9. **c.**
10. **a.**
11. **b.**

Canada

Quiz 2 – More trivia

1. In 1915, a Canadian bear cub named Winnipeg was sent to the London Zoo.

   a) The cub later served in the English Army during the Great War.

   b) A. A. Milne, whose son Christopher Robin loved to visit Winnipeg, authored Winnie-the-Pooh.

   c) The cub was adopted by Winston Churchill in 1916.

2. The Canadian motto, '*A Mari Usque ad Mare*', means

   a) 'The bears are our friends'.

   b) 'From sea to sea'.

   c) 'Diversity is power'.

3. Canada was invaded by the USA.

   a) False.

   b) True, in 1812.

   c) True, in 1775 and in 1812.

4. Canada holds the record for winning the most Winter Olympics gold medals (at the 2010 Vancouver Winter Olympics). Team Canada tallied

   a) 12 medals.

   b) 14 medals.

c) 16 medals.

5. A building in Rodney, Ontario, measures just 4.5 m by 5.4 m (14.7 feet by 17.7 feet) and is Canada's smallest
   a) university.
   b) jail.
   c) hospital.

6. The Canadian flag is called
   a) The Maple Leaf or l'Unifolié.
   b) The White-Red Banner or Rouge-blanc.
   c) The Flag or Le drapeau.

7. In 1962, Pincher Creek, Alberta, saw the fastest temperature change ever recorded in Canada: from $-19°$ Celsius to $+22°$ Celsius ($-2°$ Fahrenheit to $+72°$ Fahrenheit) within
   a) 10 minutes.
   b) a single hour.
   c) three hours.

8. The village Alert, Nunavut Territory, is the world's northernmost
   a) ski resort.
   b) ice camp.
   c) permanent settlement.

9. Della Falls, British Columbia, with its 440 m (1443 feet) drop is the highest waterfall in
   a) Canada.
   b) North America.
   c) the world.

10. Estevan, Saskatchewan, is known to be Canada's
    a) sunniest place.
    b) largest port.
    c) gambling capital.

Answers:

1. **b.**
2. **b.**

3. **c.**
4. **b.**
5. **b.**
6. **a.**
7. **b.**
8. **c.**
9. **a.**
10. **a.** *It has on average 2400 sunshine hours every year.*

Canada
Quiz 3 – Surprising facts

1. Canada's national summer sport is
   a) hockey.
   b) football.
   c) lacrosse.

2. In 1921, insulin was first isolated at the University of
   a) Montreal.
   b) Vancouver.
   c) Toronto.

3. The Rideau Canal in Ottawa is the world's longest
   a) freshwater canal.
   b) naturally frozen ice ring.
   c) manmade construction.

4. Canada's beaver is the second largest rodent in the world weighing up to 35 kg (70 pounds). It is surpassed only by the
   a) European beaver.
   b) capybara.
   c) Laotian giant flying squirrel.

5. On 30 May 1961, 250 mm (10 inches) rain fell in Buffalo Gap, Saskatchewan, in less than

a) an hour.

b) two hours.

c) three hours.

6. Worldwide, Canada is the largest producer of
a) caesium.

b) petrol.

c) silver.

7. Santa Claus was officially granted Canadian citizenship in
a) 1987.

b) 2001.

c) 2010.

8. In Canada, pre-employment drug tests are
a) against the law.

b) mandatory for all.

c) mandatory for immigrants only.

9. On average, there is a suicide attempt at Niagara Falls every
a) day.

b) week.

c) month.

Answers:

1. **c.**
2. **c.**
3. **b.**
4. **b.** *The top recorded weight is 91 kg (201 pounds) for a wild female capybara.*

5. **a.**
6. **a.**
7. **c.**
8. **a.**
9. **b.**

Canada

Quiz 4 – Which is NOT true about Canada?

1. Which is false?
   a) In the early 11th century, Snorri Thorfinnsson was born in Vinland (the Vikings' name for Newfoundland). He was probably the first Caucasian child born in the New World.
   b) In Quebec, it is illegal to deny the existence of God.
   c) The capital Ottawa was originally named Bytown after Colonel John By.

2. Which is false?
   a) Statistically, a car accident involving a moose occurs every day.
   b) Comics depicting criminal activities are outlawed in Canada.
   c) In Vancouver, more than eight women may not live in the same house because it would be deemed to constitute a brothel.

3. Which is false?
   a) Canada comprises ten provinces and three territories.
   b) French and English are both official languages in Canada.

c) More than 90 percent of Canadians are English-French bilingual.

4. Which is false?

a) Six cities in Canada have a population of over one million: Toronto, Montreal, Vancouver, Calgary, Edmonton and Ottawa.

b) Canadians are not permitted to carry weapons.

c) Technically, Queen Elizabeth II is still the official Head of State.

5. Which is false?

a) Canada has about 10 percent of the world's forests (covering half of its territory). It also has almost 10 percent of the world's renewable water supply.

b) The longest highway worldwide is the Trans-Canada Highway, stretching over 8000 km (5000 miles).

c) The game of ice-hockey is depicted on all banknotes.

6. Which is false?

a) Hockey is the national sport since the late 1890s.

b) The world's northernmost sand dunes are in Athabasca Provincial Park, Saskatchewan.

c) The highest peak in Canada is Mount Logan, 5959 m (19 551 feet).

7. Which is false?

   a) The Blackberry smartphones were developed in Ontario.

   b) The Big Nickel in Sudbury, Ontario, measures 9 m (30 feet) in diameter and is the world's largest coin in circulation.

   c) The Mounted Police were established in 1873.

8. Which is false?

   a) Canada's only desert is 23 km (15 miles) long and is the only desert in the world with a boardwalk for visitors.

   b) In Canada, all prescription drugs and long-term health care are free.

   c) It snows three out of every four days at Mount Fidelity, Glacier National Park, British Columbia. Each year, this place sees more than 10 m (400 inches) of snow.

9. Which is false?

   a) British Columbian pioneers used to burn the small fish oolichan, also called eulachon or candlefish, at night. It is so fatty that it can be dried out and burnt like a candle.

   b) Every year, tens of thousands of red-sided garter snakes gather at the Narcisse Snake Dens in Manitoba.

   c) In Canada, officially the plural of moose is 'meese'.

10. Which is false?

    a) In Montreal, a man with a moustache may never kiss a woman in public.

    b) There are no snakes on the entire island of Newfoundland.

    c) Canada officially got its own national flag in 1965 — almost a century after it became a country.

by Nayden Kostov

Answers:

1. **b.**
2. **c.** *It is true however in many places in the USA.*
3. **c.** *The real number is more like 18 percent.*
4. **b.**
5. **c.** *Hockey is present on Canadian five-dollar note though.*

6. **a.** *Since its founding, Canada's official sport was lacrosse. In 1994, First Nations groups objected to a government bill that proposed establishing ice hockey as Canada's national sport, arguing that it neglected recognition of the game of lacrosse, a uniquely Native contribution. In response, the House of Commons amended a bill 'to recognize hockey as Canada's Winter Sport and lacrosse as Canada's Summer Sport,' although lacrosse is played all year, in all seasons, indoor and outdoors. On 12 May 1994, the National Sports of Canada Act came into force with these designations.*
7. **b.**
8. **b.** *The Canada Health Act does not cover prescription drugs, home care or long-term care, prescription glasses or dental care, which means most Canadians pay out-of-pocket for these services or rely on private insurance.*
9. **c.**
10. **a.** *However, it is reportedly the case in Iowa, USA.*

Canada

Quiz 5 – Some more questions
(Which is NOT true?)

1. Which is false?

    a) In Dawson City, Yukon, anyone can join the 'Sourtoe Cocktail Club'. The entrance test involves finishing a drink with a real human toe at the bottom of the glass.

    b) In Canada, liquor stores may not place advertisements outside the store.

    c) Until 2008, it was illegal to sell carbonated drinks in cans in Prince Edward Island. Only refillable glass bottles were allowed.

2. Which is false?

    a) The electromagnet was invented in Calgary.

    b) Ogopogo is the name of a mysterious lake creature that reportedly lives in Lake Okanagan, British Columbia.

    c) The coldest temperature ever recorded in Canada was in Snag, Yukon. It was $-63°$ Celsius ($-81.4°$ Fahrenheit).

3. Which is false?

    a) The border between Canada and the USA stretches an amazing 8891 km (5525 miles). It is officially dubbed the International Boundary and is world's longest unprotected border.

b) It rains nine out of ten days in Ocean Falls, British Columbia.

   c) Cat's eye road markings were invented by a former Canadian Minister of Transport.

4. Which is false?

   a) Nunavut is four times larger than France and covers 21 percent of Canada's total land area.

   b) Calgary is famous for its chinooks (warm, dry winds from the Rocky Mountains) that can raise the temperature by 10 degrees in a matter of minutes.

   c) The population of Canada is about 60 million people.

5. Which is false?

   a) All dog food is tax-deductible in Canada.

   b) 90 percent of Canada's population lives within 160 km (100 miles) of the US border.

   c) The average life expectancy is over 81 years.

6. Which is false?

   a) Many Canadians finish their sentences with the word *'eh'*.

   b) There have been twenty-five Canadian Nobel Prize laureates.

   c) The first SMS message in the world was sent in Canada.

7. Which is false?

   a) Canada has hosted three Olympic Games: the 1976 Montreal Games, the 1988 Calgary Games and the 2010 Vancouver Games.

   b) Canadian inventions include the telephone, basketball, snowmobile, electric cooking range and baseball glove.

   c) In 1912, a Canadian pilot threw the world's first purpose-built air-to-surface bomb from an airplane.

8. Which is false?

   a) Canada produces ice wine made from pressed frozen grapes.

   b) The first bone marrow transplant was performed in Ottawa.

   c) Canada holds the world record for doughnut shops per capita.

9. Which is false?

   a) The first professional basketball game was played in Toronto, Canada: Toronto Huskies vs New York Knicks.

   b) Royal Bank of Canada's HQ building in Toronto has windows tinted with pure gold.

   c) Edmonton is the first town in the world where Aspirin could be bought. They have been selling the painkiller since 1853.

10. Which is false?

    a) Half of all polar bears in the world live in Nunavut.

    b) The Bank of Canada issued its first bank notes in 1935. At the time, the bank was a privately owned corporation.

    c) Ping pong used to be prohibited in Canada. It was believed that playing the game damaged people's eyesight.

11. Which is false?

    a) Wasaga Beach, Ontario, is the longest freshwater beach in the world.

    b) Manitoulin Island is the largest freshwater island in the world.

    c) The West Edmonton Mall is the largest shopping mall in the world.

by Nayden Kostov

Answers:

1. **b.**

2. **a.** *In fact, the electromagnet was invented in the UK by William Sturgeon (22 May 1783 – 4 December 1850).*

3. **c.** *The inventor of cat's eyes was Percy Shaw (15 April 1890 – 1 September 1976) of Boothtown, Halifax, West Yorkshire, England.*

4. **c.** *Canada has a population of 35 million.*

5. **a.** *Not all dog food. It only qualifies as a tax deduction for owners of guide dogs or outdoor dogs that protect farm crops and herds.*

6. **c.** *SMS messaging was used for the first time in the UK on 3 December 1992, when Neil Papworth, a 22-year-old test engineer used a personal computer to send the text message 'Merry Christmas' to a phone.*

7. **c.** *In 1912, during the First Balkan War, Bulgarian Air Force pilot Christo Toprakchiev suggested the use of aircraft to drop 'bombs' (called grenades in the Bulgarian army at this time) on Turkish positions. On 16 October 1912, observer Prodan Tarakchiev dropped two of those bombs on the Turkish railway station of Karağaç (near the besieged Edirne) from an Albatros F.2 aircraft piloted by Radul Milkov, for the first time in this campaign. This is deemed to be the first use of an aircraft as a bomber.*

8. **b.** *Dr. Robert A. Good performed the first successful bone marrow transplant in 1968 at the University of Minnesota, USA.*

9. **c.** *Aspirin was developed by the German company Bayer AG at the very end of the 19th century.*

10. **c.** *Table tennis was banned in the Soviet Union from 1930 to 1950. The sport was believed to be harmful to the eyes.*

11. **c.** *The West Edmonton Mall (photo below) is the largest shopping mall in North America.*

Canada

Quiz 6 – Even more crazy questions
(Which is NOT true?)

1. Which is false?
   a) Buddhism is the second most widespread religion in Canada.
   b) Saskatchewan does not follow daylight savings time.
   c) The license plates for cars, snowmobiles and motor-bikes in Nunavut were shaped in the form of a polar bear until 2012.

2. Which is false?
   a) Ironically, Newfoundland was the first part of Canada to be explored by Europeans and the last to become a province. It only joined the Canadian Confederation in 1949.
   b) Newfoundland is nicknamed 'The Rock'.
   c) In the southernmost parts of Newfoundland, many farmers cultivate lemons.

3. Which is false?
   a) The USA buys more oil from Canada than from any other country.
   b) Knives should not be offered as gifts in Canada. The gesture is considered to be provocative and offensive.

c) People in Churchill, Manitoba, leave their cars unlocked so as to allow their neighbours to hide in them in the event of an encounter with a polar bear.

4. Which is false?
   a) Four species of primates are indigenous to Canada.
   b) Canadian cows are not given artificial hormones.
   c) In 1943, Ottawa declared for a day a hospital room to be 'extraterritorial' so as to allow a Dutch princess to be born on Dutch soil.

5. Which is false?
   a) The quality of tap water in Canada is better than bottled water in many countries.
   b) A Canadian F-15 fighter jet once lost a wing whilst out on patrol but nevertheless managed to land safely at Montreal Airport.
   c) In 2007, the Canadian Mint created a 1 000 000 Canadian dollars coin. The coin can be used as legal tender.

6. Which is false?
   a) At the 1930 World Ice Hockey Championships, the Canadian national team automatically acceded to the final without having to play through knockout stages. They proceeded to trounce their opponents.
   b) Every year, millions of letters addressed to 'Santa

Claus, North Pole' arrive in Canada. Post office volunteers respond to each one, signing them 'Santa Claus, North Pole, H0H 0H0'.

c) Canada produces 98 percent of the world's pure maple syrup.

7. Which is false?

a) During the holiday seasons, a volunteer service called 'Operation Red Nose' gives free rides to those too drunk to drive.

b) Canada has an official phone number. It is 1-800-O-Canada.

c) In Toronto, tattooing was illegal until 1979. The offense was punishable by severe penalties including jail sentences.

8. Which is false?

a) A Canadian comedian died of a heart attack on live television midway through an act in 1984. The audience continued applauding assuming it to be part of the performance.

b) A man from Ontario invented the Hawaiian pizza.

c) Canada keeps a strategic maple syrup reserve.

9. Which is false?

a) Alberta is the only province in Canada that is rat-free.

b) Canada switched to right-hand street traffic in 1964.

c) There is actually an island in Canada called Dildo Island.

10. Which is false?

a) Up until 2015, the McLobster sandwich could only be purchased at McDonald's restaurants in Canada.

b) One can study 'The Science of Batman' at the University of Victoria.

c) The first ever cup of hot chocolate was served in Quebec.

11. Which is false?

a) The gravity in Hudson Bay region is slightly weaker than in the rest of the world. Scientists are still unable to properly explain the phenomenon.

b) In Canada, prostitution is not and has never been illegal.

c) The first commercial popcorn machine was invented by Mr Charles Cretors in Toronto at the end of the 19th century.

by Nayden Kostov

Answers:

1. **a.**
2. **c.**
3. **b.**
4. **a.** *Of all primates, only humans are indigenous to Canada.*
5. **b.** *In 1983, an Israeli Air Force F-15 (photo below) was able to land with one wing in the Negev desert, in Israel.*

6. **c.** *Canada produces 'only' around 80 percent of the world's pure maple syrup.*
7. **c.**
8. **a.** *It was the Welsh comedian Tommy Cooper who died of a heart attack on live television midway through an act.*
9. **b.**
10. **c.**
11. **c.** *Charles Cretors originated from Lebanon, Ohio (USA). He travelled the Midwest and settled in Fort Scott, Kansas, for a few years, and then Decatur, Illinois.*

Various countries

Quiz 1 – How much do you know about the countries in the world?

1. Which country is the heaviest consumer of beer per capita in the world?
   a) Czech Republic
   b) Germany
   c) Australia

2. Nodding your head expresses *'yes'* in the vast majority of cultures. Be careful though as it means *'no'* in
   a) Sweden.
   b) Finland.
   c) Bulgaria.

3. The full official name of Romania is
   a) 'Romania'.
   b) 'Republic of Romania'.
   c) 'Romanian Republic'.

4. Where are 3-euro coins in circulation?
   a) Nowhere
   b) Slovenia
   c) Spain

5. Neckties were first used in

a) Croatia.

b) France.

c) Italy.

6. Women or larger-than-cat female animals are not allowed in one part of which European country?

a) Hungary

b) Wales

c) Greece

7. In 1712, there was a 30 February in

a) Sweden.

b) the Netherlands.

c) the Russian Empire.

8. Which European country could not form a government for almost two years?

a) France

b) Belgium

c) Italy

9. Flushing the toilet after 10 pm is against the law in some districts of which European country?

a) Belarus.

b) Switzerland.

c) Moldova.

10. The deepest metro station in the world is in

a) Hungary.

b) Great Britain.

c) Ukraine.

Answers:

1. **a.**
2. **c.**

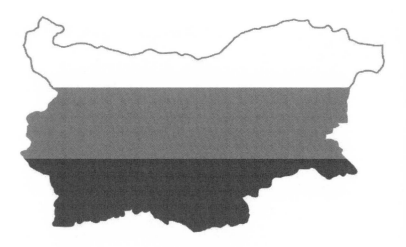

3. **a.**
4. **b.**
5. **a.**
6. **c.**
7. **a.**
8. **b.**
9. **b.**
10. **c.** *Arsenalna is a station on Kiev Metro's Sviatoshyns-ko-Brovarska Line. The station is currently the deepest station in the world — 106 m (347 feet).*

Various countries

Quiz 2 – How much do you know about the countries in the world?

1. In Norway, one in four cars is
   a) white.
   b) electric.
   c) over 350 horsepower.

2. Saudi Arabia banned Pokémon cards because
   a) believers got distracted and kept forgetting to pray.
   b) of fears that the game encouraged Zionism.
   c) there was no Muslim Pokémon depicted.

3. Worldwide, the Republic of Guyana has the highest
   a) GDP per capita.
   b) number of bridges per capita.
   c) suicide rate.

4. The Ford Pinto was not a success in Brazil. *'Pinto'* in local slang means:
   a) *'small penis'*.
   b) *'small brain'*.
   c) *'small biceps'*.

5. The only NATO member without an army is
   a) Costa Rica.

b) Switzerland.

   c) Iceland.

6. Brussels became the *'capital'* of the European Union because

   a) it was first in the alphabetical list and at the time it was thought to be a temporary solution.

   b) it was the candidate that was located farthest from the Communist countries' armies.

   c) at the time, it had the best airport.

7. Which country has four official languages and uses none of them on its postage stamps?

   a) Aruba

   b) Chile

   c) Switzerland

8. The sun is considered red in Japan and yellow/orange in the Western world but from space it looks

   a) white.

   b) blueish.

   c) red/orange.

9. In 1967, a country in Europe changed its street traffic directionality from left (UK style) to right (continental style). The very first day, traffic was a total mess. It happened in

a) Ireland.

b) Sweden.

c) Liechtenstein.

10. The Arabic numerals actually originated in

a) China.

b) India.

c) Persia.

Answers:

1. **b.**
2. **b.** *Do not ask me how…*
3. **c.** *As of 2015.*
4. **a.**
5. **c.**
6. **a.**
7. **c.** *They use Latin.*

8. **a.**
9. **b.**
10. **b.** *The Hindu-Arabic numerals were invented by mathematicians in India. Perso-Arabic mathematicians called them 'Hindu numerals' (where 'Hindu' meant Indian). Later they came to be called 'Arabic numerals' in Europe, because they were introduced to the West by Arab merchants.*

Various countries

Quiz 3 – How much do you know about the countries in the world?

1. Scissors were invented in
   a) Ancient Egypt.
   b) China.
   c) India.

2. Many Chinese women wear bathing suits that cover their face. Why?
   a) They are afraid of local parasites.
   b) They are ashamed of their body and do not want to be recognised.
   c) In China, suntan on the face is often associated with peasantry and is, therefore, undesirable.

3. Which African country has far more pyramids than Egypt?
   a) Sudan
   b) Ethiopia
   c) Morocco

4. Until 2011, beer was not considered an alcoholic drink in
   a) Germany.
   b) Russia.
   c) Czech Republic.

5. The largest football stadium in Europe is
   a) Wembley, England.
   b) Camp Nou, Spain.
   c) Santiago Bernabéu, Spain.

6. Women in Vatican
   a) cannot vote.
   b) cannot drive.
   c) cannot open a bank account.

7. The only country with a non-rectangular flag is
   a) Nepal.
   b) Mongolia.
   c) Belize.

8. Until 1980, Rhodesia was the name of today's
   a) Zimbabwe.
   b) Congo.
   c) Somalia.

9. There is a national anthem of a European country saying 'The king of Spain I have always honoured'. And no, it is not the Spanish one. It is the anthem of
   a) Portugal.
   b) Andorra.
   c) The Netherlands.

Answers:

1. **a.**
2. **c.**

3. **a.**
4. **b.**
5. **b.** *It is located in the city of Barcelona.*
6. **a.**
7. **a.**
8. **a.**
9. **c.**

CHAPTER II

MISCELLANEOUS

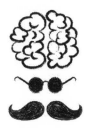

Quiz 1 – Various animals

1. Which animal has fingerprints that cannot be easily distinguished from human ones?
   a) Panda
   b) Koala
   c) Racoon

2. Rudolf, Santa's reindeer, is depicted wrong in most Christmas pictures and movies. Why?
   a) The shape of the nose.
   b) The shape of the hooves.
   c) Rudolf has to be a girl.

3. Which colour are the new-born lady bugs?
   a) Yellow
   b) White
   c) Red

4. Winnie-the-Pooh was named after
   a) the author's children.
   b) the dog Winnie and the cat Pooh.
   c) the bear Winnie and the swan Pooh.

5. The platypus is the only
   a) egg-laying mammal.

b) mammal with a venomous spur.

c) hermaphrodite mammal.

6. Pink flamingos are born

a) white.

b) yellow.

c) pink.

by Nayden Kostov

Answers:

1. **b.**

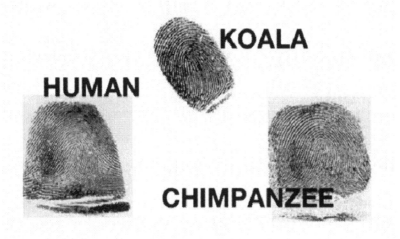

2. **c.** Male reindeer lose their antlers before Christmas, while females do not.
3. **a.**
4. **c.**
5. **b.**
6. **a.**

Quiz 2 – Pig trivia

1. In the early 1990s, out of roughly two billion pigs in the world, how many were there in Afghanistan?

a) 1

b) 50

c) 300

2. Until the very end of the 20th century they would feed pigs in Bhutan with

a) used motor oil.

b) poppy seeds.

c) cannabis.

3. Pigs have

a) 34 teeth.

b) 44 teeth.

c) 54 teeth.

4. A sow's pregnancy lasts 114 days and can occur twice a year. Each time, it can give birth to between

a) 1 and 3 piglets.

b) 4 and 6 piglets.

c) 7 and 12 piglets.

5. At birth a piglet weighs about 1.5 kg (3 pounds) and only a week later –

a) up to 50 percent more.

b) up to two times more.

c) up to three times more.

6. The words *pig*, *hog* and *swine* can be used regardless of the

a) age.

b) size.

c) gender.

7. Piglets respond to their names at the age of

a) 20 days.

b) 40 days.

c) 60 days.

8. Pigs can run at a top speed of

a) 10 km/h (6 mph).

b) 20 km/h (12 mph).

c) 30 km/h (18 mph).

9. Pigs roll around in the mud to

a) lower their body temperature as they have no sweat glands.

b) get rid of the fleas.

c) massage their backs.

10. Pig skin, being similar to human skin, is great for practicing

a) massages.

b) tattoos.

c) make-up techniques.

11. Pigs have 4 toes on each hoof. For walking, they only use
   a) one of them.
   b) two of them.
   c) three of them.

12. Pigs have a remarkable sense of smell and are used to locate
   a) truffles.
   b) drugs.
   c) dead bodies.

Answers:

1. **a.** *The Taliban regime was not very fond of pigs.*
2. **c.**
3. **b.**
4. **c.**

5. **b.**
6. **c.**
7. **a.**
8. **b.**
9. **a.**
10. **b.** *Not that great for the pigs, though.*
11. **b.**
12. **a.**

Quiz 3 – Pig trivia (Which is NOT true?)

1. Which is false?
   a) There are many documented stories of pigs that saved human lives.
   b) Pigs were successfully used against Hannibal's war elephants. A shrieking pig can freak out any elephant.
   c) Pigs have significantly fewer taste receptors than humans.

2. Which is false?
   a) 'Mini pig' is a real breed of pigs.
   b) Genetically, pigs are not much different from us. Thus transplantation of pig heart valves to humans is possible.
   c) The words sucker, weaner, baconer, porker, chopper, sow, boar, piglet and stag all refer to pigs.

3. Which is false?
   a) Pigs never shed their hair.
   b) Pigs are quite intelligent and learn tricks faster than dogs.
   c) Pigs have a vast field of vision, but cannot look up.

4. Which is false?
   a) Pigs' intelligence is inferior only to some apes, dolphins and elephants.

b) Pigs are immune to snake bites.

c) Pigs communicate with each other by grunting.

5. Which is false?

a) Pigs swim just fine and would eagerly prefer water to mud.

b) There is a word to designate a litter of piglets – a 'farrow'.

c) Pigs will eat anything.

6. Which is false?

a) The pig is part of the Chinese zodiac and is believed to bring fortune and happiness.

b) All pigs have curly tails.

c) Pigs actually like being clean. They never establish a toilet area close to where they lie and eat.

Answers:

1. **c.** *Compared to humans, pigs have 3-4 times more taste buds.*
2. **a.**
3. **a.**
4. **b.**
5. **c.**
6. **b.**

Quiz 4 – Pandas are amazing

1. The word *'panda'* is derived from the Nepalese *'poonya'*, meaning
   a) *'bamboo-eating animal'*.
   b) *'black and white'*.
   c) *'friendly ghost'*.

2. The giant panda is so close to extinction that it is referred to as a
   a) *'Lazarus species'*.
   b) *'living fossil'*.
   c) *'Dodo'*.

3. Male pandas have
   a) more fingers on their paws than females.
   b) a bone inside their penis.
   c) fewer black spots than female pandas.

4. Every year, the entire mating period lasts about
   a) a few hours.
   b) a couple of days.
   c) two weeks.

5. Cubs are raised by
   a) both parents.

b) the female panda only.

c) several female pandas.

6. If a panda has twins, the weaker cub

a) receives more attention.

b) is given to a childless female panda for *'adoption'*.

c) is normally not going to survive.

7. Pandas in captivity have

a) twins more often.

b) fewer black spots.

c) thicker fur.

8. Many new-born pandas die from

a) starvation.

b) being accidentally crushed by their mothers.

c) cannibalism.

9. Unlike other bears, pandas do not

a) hibernate.

b) mark their territory.

c) have molar teeth.

10. The panda is blind for the first

a) two days of its life.

b) two weeks of its life.

c) two months of its life.

Answers:

1. **a.**
2. **b.**

3. **b.**
4. **b.**
5. **b.**
6. **c.**
7. **a.**
8. **b.**
9. **a.**
10. **c.**

by Nayden Kostov

Quiz 5 – Panda trivia

1. Pandas are born
   a) all-white.
   b) black and white.
   c) all-black.

2. Out of over 130 bamboo species, pandas only eat
   a) 25.
   b) 40.
   c) 65.

3. Every day, a panda eats up to
   a) 7 kg (15 pounds) of bamboo shoots.
   b) 12 kg (25 pounds) of bamboo shoots.
   c) 20 kg (45 pounds) of bamboo shoots.

4. Pandas spend most of their time (up to 14 hours a day)
   a) sleeping.
   b) looking for food.
   c) eating.

5. The red panda is not a real panda. It belongs to the
   a) raccoon family.
   b) dog family.
   c) lemur family.

6. Pandas mark territory by rubbing their scent glands onto a tree. These are located
   a) behind the ears.
   b) under the tail.
   c) in the armpits.

7. Pandas' skin is black where its fur is black. Where its fur is white, the skin below is
   a) white.
   b) pink.
   c) brown.

8. An adult panda weighs up to
   a) 100 kg (220 pounds).
   b) 140 kg (310 pounds).
   c) 190 kg (420 pounds).

9. Pandas are the most expensive animals in a zoo. The second most expensive animals are
   a) elephants.
   b) rhinoceroses.
   c) lions.

10. The first live panda left China in
    a) 1768.
    b) 1835.
    c) 1936.

Answers:

1. **a.**
2. **a.**
3. **c.**
4. **c.**
5. **a.**

6. **b.**
7. **b.**
8. **b.**
9. **a.**
10. **c.** *For centuries, people outside China thought that the giant panda was simply a legend and not a real animal.*

Quiz 6 – Latin Dances trivia and surprising facts

1. Bruce Lee perfectly danced Latin Dances and at the age of 18 years became Hong Kong's Champion in
   a) Cha Cha.
   b) Samba.
   c) Rumba.

2. Which of the following is not of Cuban origin?
   a) Cha Cha
   b) Mambo
   c) Merengue

3. Despite both being called Latin dances, Paso Doble actually originated in Spain and Jive came from
   a) the UK.
   b) the USA.
   c) Canada.

4. The slowest among all Latin dances is
   a) Rumba.
   b) Bolero.
   c) Paso Doble.

5. Which of the following is not of Dominican origin?
   a) Merengue

b) Rumba

c) Bachata

6. Until the early 1990s, when it turned towards more romantic lyrics, which dance was associated mostly with crime and prostitution, and just one national radio station would play it?

a) Bachata

b) Merengue

c) Kizomba

7. In 1989, which dance started in Angola and became extremely popular in all Portuguese speaking countries?

a) Kizomba

b) Salsa Mbalax

c) Bachata

8. In 1913, which dance became the one that virtually everybody worldwide wanted to learn?

a) Jive

b) Paso Doble

c) Tango

9. The solo breaks during the performance are known as

a) *'solos'*.

b) *'shines'*.

c) *'spotlights'*.

10. The solo form of Salsa (the line dancing) is called

a) Salsa Suelta.

b) Salsa Solo.

c) Salsa Uno.

11. In which Salsa style dancers stick very close to each other while performing tight spins and unbelievably fast foot-work?

a) Cuban.

b) New York.

c) Cali.

12. In which Salsa style are there lots of shines and show-offs?

a) L.A.

b) Miami

c) Cuban

13. The Cuban genre of music Salsa Cubana is actually called

a) Casino.

b) Salsa.

c) Timba.

14. The movie 'Dance with Me' first featured

a) Miami style Salsa.

b) New York style.

c) Cuban Salsa (Rueda).

15. Santiago de Cali, Colombia, is known as the

a) 'Capital de la Salsa'.

b) 'Birthplace of Salsa'.

c) 'Home of Salsa'.

16. In the US, Salsa dance had its peak of popularity in the 1970s, coinciding with

a) a governmental attempt to divert the public attention from the Watergate scandal by extensively subsidising ethnic music events.

b) the fact that many protesters against the Vietnam War danced it in front of the White House.

c) the influx of many Dominican and Puerto Rican immigrants.

Answers:

1. **a.**

2. **c.**
3. **b.**
4. **b.**
5. **b.**
6. **a.**
7. **a.**
8. **c.**
9. **b.**
10. **a.**

11. **c.**
12. **b.**
13. **c.**
14. **c.**
15. **a.**
16. **c.**

Quiz 7 – Truly random questions

1. How many musical instruments are required in order to use the term *'big band'*?
   a) 14
   b) 35
   c) 56

2. The first product to have a bar code was
   a) a Mars dessert bar.
   b) a tube of toothpaste.
   c) a Wrigley's gum.

3. What do Yoda and Miss Piggy have in common?
   a) The characters of Yoda and Miss Piggy were voiced by the same person.
   b) The puppets were produced by the same company.
   c) Yoda means *'pig'* in Zulu dialect.

4. The Hundred Year's War actually lasted
   a) 100 years.
   b) 116 years.
   c) 123 years.

5. Rick Allen, the drummer of Def Leppard, is unlike any other drummer of a famous band. Why?
   a) He is deaf.

b) He is blind.

c) He has only one hand.

6. The word *'dreamt'* is peculiar because

   a) in English, it is the only one (excluding derivatives) that ends with 'mt'.

   b) grammar experts want this form abolished and changed to 'dreamed'.

   c) the majority of US first-graders spell it wrong.

7. Molotov cocktails were named after

   a) an actual Soviet minister of foreign affairs.

   b) their inventor.

   c) a Soviet guerrilla commander who first used one.

8. A 2HB pencil can draw a continuous line of roughly

   a) 5 km (3 miles).

   b) 50 km (30 miles).

   c) 500 km (300 miles).

9. How many people climbed Mount Everest in 2015?

   a) 0

   b) 6

   c) 12

10. The encircled 'U' on food labels means that

    a) it is kosher.

    b) it does not contain GMO.

    c) it is halal.

11. In black and white TV era, female anchors used lipstick and make up in two strange colours.

    a) Green and black

    b) Violet and orange

    c) Blue and brown

Answers:

1. **a.**
2. **c.**
3. **a.** *Frank Oz is an English-born American puppeteer, film-maker and actor. He voiced both.*
4. **b.**
5. **c.**

6. **a.**
7. **a.** *Vyacheslav Mikhailovich Molotov (9 March 1890 – 8 November 1986) was a Soviet politician and diplomat, an Old Bolshevik, and a leading figure in the Soviet government from the 1920s, when he rose to power as a protégé of Joseph Stalin. Molotov was the principal Soviet signatory of the Nazi–Soviet non-aggression pact of 1939 (also known as the Molotov–Ribbentrop Pact), whose most important provisions were added in the form of a secret protocol that stipulated an invasion of Poland and partition of its territory between Germany and the Soviet Union.*
8. **b.**
9. **a.** *There was a devastating earthquake in the region in 2015 which foiled all climbing attempts.*
10. **a.**
11. **a.**

Quiz 8 – More truly random questions

1. The holes in pen caps are there

   a) to save people from choking to death.

   b) purely for design.

   c) to prevent the ink from drying.

2. Some shopping centres and restaurants play classical music in their car parks at night to

   a) make it more pleasant for the pedestrians passing by.

   b) stop teenagers from gathering there.

   c) promote culture.

3. Can a triangle have 3 right angles?

   a) Yes, if drawn on a sphere.

   b) Yes, if using the 4th dimension.

   c) Impossible.

4. Which colour did Homer not mention in *'The Odyssey'*?

   a) Yellow

   b) Blue

   c) Green

5. In the Solar System, there is only one planet that turns clockwise. It is

   a) Mercury.

b) Venus.

c) Jupiter.

6. *'Checkmate'* literally means

a) *'the victory is mine'.*

b) *'the king is dead'.*

c) *'now you surrender'.*

7. Pink peppercorns are not like green, black or white peppercorns. Why?

a) They are artificially coloured.

b) They are not allowed to the US market.

c) They are not real peppercorns but berries of the Brazilian pepper tree.

8. Lamborghini models are often named after

a) famous corrida bulls.

b) nicknames of professional wrestlers.

c) mythical creatures.

9. Before he decided he could make better cars than Ferrari, Ferruccio Lamborghini was producing and is still producing

a) trucks.

b) tractors.

c) boats.

10. Which letter is not used in the Periodic Table?

   a) Y

   b) J

   c) Q

11. The airline company flying to the largest number of countries is

   a) Turkish Airlines.

   b) Emirates.

   c) Lufthansa.

Answers:

1. **a.**
2. **b.**
3. **a.**

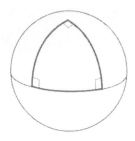

4. **b.** *Blue does not appear at all in Greek stories and other ancient written texts. Egyptians were the first civilisation to have a word for the colour blue around 2500 BC.*
5. **b.**
6. **b.**
7. **c.**
8. **a.**
9. **b.**

10. **b.**
11. **a.**

BONUS – FACTS FROM MY NEXT BOOK

- Norwegians use the word 'Texas' as a synonym to 'crazy'.
- Astronauts use diapers during take-off and landing and while on space walks.
- There are freshwater sharks in Lake Nicaragua, Nicaragua.
- The famous Italian painter, Caravaggio, committed murder.
- In Italy, the number 17 is considered unlucky.
- Celluloid billiards balls can literally explode on impact.
- Jupiter and Saturn radiate more energy than they absorb from the sun.
- Pistachios can combust spontaneously.
- Centipedes never have exactly 100 legs.
- Cockatoos sometimes eat so much that they lose the ability to fly for a certain period.
- Mickey Mouse was the first non-human to win an Oscar.
- Early blindness prevents schizophrenia. Not a single case has ever been reported among people born blind or having lost their eyesight as infants.
- The first hybrid car was built one century earlier than what you most probably think. In 1898, it was patented under the name 'System Lohner-Porsche'.
- Ostriches need to raise their head in order to swallow when eating and drinking.

- The Hague is the third biggest inhabited locality in the Netherlands with its 510 000 citizens. Administratively speaking however, it has never received an official city status and is dubbed 'the largest village in Europe'.

- In 1927, Julius Wagner-Jauregg received a Nobel Prize for his discovery that if one had syphilis and then contracted malaria, the high fever would cure the syphilis.

- Twelve publishing houses rejected J. K. Rowling's 'Harry Potter' before it got published; William Golding's 'Lord of the Flies' was rejected twenty times.

- Out of superstition, Japanese avoid cutting their nails after dark. Nor do they whistle at night.

- After sexual intercourse, men's beards grow faster.

VERIFICATION PROCESS

To start with, however a great read Wikipedia is, I have **never** used it to confirm facts; I rather checked the sources listed there and evaluated them.

Anything science-related like *'Jupiter and Saturn radiate more energy than they absorb from the sun'* would need to be confirmed by at least two (preferably three) separate scientific publications, be it on paper or online of the sort of http://www.science.gov/, http://www.nasa.gov/, http://www.britannica.com/, http://www.sciencemag.org/, https://www.newscientist.com/, https://www.genome.gov/education/, http://www.howstuffworks.com/, http://www.merriam-webster.com/. The scientific publications and websites of the best universities worldwide are also consistently checked (excerpt from the list): University of Cambridge, Stanford University, University of Oxford, California Institute of Technology, Massachusetts Institute of Technology, Harvard University, Princeton University, Imperial College London, ETH Zurich – Swiss Federal Institute of Technology, Yale University, Columbia University, University of Toronto, Humboldt University of Berlin, University of Tokyo, Heidelberg University, University of Melbourne, Peking University etc.

For events or facts of the type *'In 2001, Turkmenistan outlawed opera, ballet, video games, listening to car radios, smoking in public and long hair on men'*, I checked at least three reputable newspaper articles and/or confirmed television reports. Example for newspapers / TV channels used to verify events: The New York Times, Washington Post, Wall Street Journal, The Guardian, The Economist, Financial Times, Times of India, Le Monde, The Sydney Morning Herald, Frankfurter Allgemeine Zeitung, Bloomberg, Al Jazeera, Reuters, Associated Press, BBC, TV5 MONDE, CNN, etc.

The website of the UK Law Commission http://www.lawcom. gov.uk/ proved to be a mighty ally in debunking many UK laws myths.

If there is **only one source** or if the sources were deemed not reliable, I simply discarded the fact. Exception: when NASA says that there is liquid water on Mars, I take this first-hand information as plausible. Cross-checking is not possible for the time being as all other sources also quote NASA.

by Nayden Kostov

ACKNOWLEDGEMENTS

This book is dedicated to my family: my loving wife Anna, my curious and restless sons Pavel and Nikolay, and my mother Maria, who sparked my interest in reading. Thank you for being so patient with me during the lengthy process of writing. You are my inspiration!

Many thanks to the editors Jonathon Tabet and Andrea Leitenberger; the illustrator Yuliya Krumova; to all test readers, friends, and colleagues who provided vital feedback and constructive criticism.

I am truly impressed by the Kickstarter community, which not only was great in the crowdfunding part, but also provided guidance and shared precious experience.

Zealous test readers:
Alexandra Oliveira-Jones
Alexandre Berger
Agnes Bannink
Ankit
Gergana Nikolova
Laura Perkins
Seow Wan Yi
Sonia Leonardo
Svetoslav Sabev
Sylvia Skabrina
Todd Tarbet

I hope you have enjoyed this book. I would greatly appreciate it if you would **write your honest review** on **Amazon** and/or on **GoodReads**.

You could also check out my acclaimed trivia book '1123 Hard To Believe Facts' on Amazon:

https://www.amazon.co.uk/dp/B01GQRGE6E

https://www.amazon.com/dp/B01GQRGE6E

or download a free sample from my website:

http://www.raiseyourbrain.com/1123-hard-believe-facts-e-book/

There you could also subscribe for my newsletter and learn first about my next projects.

ABOUT THE AUTHOR

Born in Bulgaria, I have lived in places like Germany, Belgium and Iraq, before settling down with my family in Luxembourg. With varied interests, I have always suffered from an insatiable appetite for facts stemming from an unrestrainable intellectual curiosity. It has certainly influenced my academic background and career: after acquiring Master degrees in Greek Philology, German and English Translation, I graduated in Crisis Management and Diplomacy and, most recently, undertook an MBA.

My career has been equally broad and diverse, swinging from that of an army paratrooper and a military intelligence analyst; through to that of a civil servant with the European Commission, and presently, that of a clerk, performing purely financial tasks in a major bank.

Member of MENSA.

WHICH IS NOT TRUE?

—

The Quiz Book

first edition

Autor: Nayden Kostov
Design: Yuliya Krumova
Format: 5,25 x 8

ISBN-13: 978-9995998035
ISBN-10: 9995998033

Made in the USA
Columbia, SC
12 February 2020